BUILDING THE CHRISTIAN ACADEMY

Building the Christian Academy

ARTHUR F. HOLMES

William B. Eerdmans Publishing Company

Grand Rapids, Michigan / Cambridge, U.K.

Wm. B. Eerdmans Publishing Co.

255 Jefferson Ave. S.E., Grand Rapids, Michigan 49503 /

P.O. Box 163, Cambridge CB3 9PU U.K.

Printed in the United States of America

05 04 03 02 01   7 6 5 4 3 2 1

Library of Congress Cataloging-in-Publication Data

Holmes, Arthur Frank, 1924-

Building the Christian academy / Arthur F. Holmes.

p.   cm.

Includes bibliographical references and index.

ISBN 0-8028-4744-7 (pbk.: alk. paper)

1. Church and education — History. 2. Education, Higher — History.

3. Education — Philosophy.   I. Title.

LA95 .H65   2001

378′.071′09 — dc21

00-066271

www.eerdmans.com

Contents

ONE

The Soul
of a University

At the conclusion of his three-volume work, *Universities of Europe in the Middle Ages,* Hastings Rashdall declares that "some knowledge of the past is a condition of practical wisdom in the present." Over the last hundred years or so, we have witnessed the progressive secularization of higher education in America and throughout the Western world, and George Marsden goes so far as to suggest that the American university has lost its soul.[1] What was that putatively Christian soul? What was it that the Christian tradition in higher education contributed that has now been lost? What should we know about that tradition as a condition of practical wisdom for the present?

Until relatively recently, the history of higher education in the West was, in fact, the story of a Christian academic tradition that played a major role in both intellectual history and the history of

---

1. George Marsden, *The Soul of the American University: From Protestant Establishment to Established Nonbelief* (New York: Oxford University Press, 1994). See also George Marsden and Bradley Longfield, eds., *The Secularization of the Academy* (New York: Oxford Univ. Press, 1992).

1

the church. To explore that story I have chosen to focus on seven formative episodes, asking in each case what problems educators faced and what major concerns guided educational thought and practice. I find four recurring emphases, which I take to be the heart and soul of the Christian academy:

1. The usefulness of liberal arts as preparation for service to both church and society
2. The unity of truth
3. Contemplative (or doxological) learning
4. The care of the soul (what we call moral and spiritual formation)

This book, then, is about the philosophy of higher education and the outworking of these four emphases in key historical contexts.[2] The concluding chapter considers the twentieth-century scenario, in which confessionally Christian colleges and universities were the closest approximation to that tradition, and affirms that we need to reclaim for our day both the four traditional emphases and the theological foundations of Christian learning.

These four emphases obviously reflect biblical influences on educational thought and practice. Consider some biblical examples of educated leaders. Moses, adopted by the princess of Egypt, had opportunities unavailable to the Hebrew people. Educated in the learning of the Egyptians and exposed to governmental leaders, he gained a sense of political responsibility and acquired thinking skills and qualities of mind that are essential for leadership. Although he retained his Hebrew identity, he spent forty years in the wilderness contemplating what he had

2. I wish to thank J. Richard Chase, who read the entire manuscript and made a number of very helpful suggestions, particularly with regard to chapter two. I addressed some of this same story in my Stob lectures, *The Soul of a Christian University* (Calvin College, 1997); discussion on that occasion confirmed the direction of the present study and forced me to sharpen the focus.

learned before God called him, a man now of both faith and learning, to lead his people. He was timid about public speaking, but demonstrated tremendous organizational skills and administrative know-how. Above all, he became the moral leader of an emerging nation in which all of life was to be lived under the guidance of God's law. Today his name is ensconced in the courtroom of the United States Supreme Court in Washington, D.C.

Think of Solomon, who at the outset of his kingly career asked not for wealth or personal honor but for wisdom to rule well and to discern good and evil. Apparently he had to work at developing that gift, for he complained that "much study is a weariness to the flesh." The first book of Kings tells us that he studied biology (both animal and plant life), wrote over a thousand songs, and collected three thousand proverbs from sources in the ancient world. Ecclesiastes indicates that he weighed and studied these proverbs and arranged them in order. That he sought "pleasing words" as well as words of truth indicates his concern about the aesthetic. Foreign rulers came to him for advice, and his decision-making amazed them. He invested in international commerce and spurred the economic development of his country. And he built a magnificent place of worship whose symbolism spoke of the overwhelming holiness of God, and whose intricate craftsmanship and artistic splendor glorified the Lord of creation. Its beauty may well have been inspired by the call we still hear to "worship the Lord in the *beauty* of holiness." But Solomon's name has stood through three millennia for wisdom, its importance, its social application, and its divine source.

And there is Daniel, "showing aptitude for every kind of learning, well informed, quick to understand, and qualified to serve in the king's palace" (Dan. 1:4).[3] He studied the language and litera-

---

3. All biblical quotations are taken from the NIV translation unless otherwise stated.

ture of the Chaldeans, and that helped him to understand not only those he served, but also himself. (Literature does that for us still.) He rejected, however, the Chaldeans' self-indulgent lifestyle and disciplined his eating habits beyond what the Mosaic dietary laws required. That kind of self-discipline helped build courage, enabling him to hold on to his Jewish faith in the face of the threat of death in the fiery furnace and in the den of lions. He risked his life in telling Nebuchadnezzar and then Belshazzar the fate awaiting them and their kingdoms, for God had entrusted him with insight into things nobody else could figure out. Daniel's name is still synonymous with courage.

The Apostle Paul grew up in the Asia Minor city of Tarsus, a university city and a center of Stoic philosophy. His writings make use of Stoic vocabulary and adapt some of its ideas, and in Athens he was able to interact with Stoic philosophers. But he was also educated as a Jewish rabbi at the feet of Gamaliel, studying the law of Moses and the wisdom of Solomon, and he doubtless read about the courage of Daniel. He became a Jewish activist, fired by faith and learning, but after his encounter with Christ he spent three years in independent study in Arabia. Inspired now by Christian understanding, he became a pioneer missionary who brought the gospel to Europe, a church planter, a missionary strategist, and a creative theologian. He was able not only to distinguish truth from error and right from wrong but also to spell out the theological and ethical implications of the gospel for both church and society in a worldview that is still valid today.

To these examples should be added the biblical literature itself — its history and rhetoric and poetry, its appreciation for music and the arts, its wisdom writings, and the prophets with their insight into the moral and religious direction of history. Not all its writers nor all its heroes had the education of a Moses, Daniel, Solomon, or Paul, for they represent a broader cross section of people, but there is clearly no incompatibility between vital faith and deep, disciplined, wide-ranging learning, between piety and hard thinking, between the life of faith and the life of the mind. Intellectual, aesthetic, and political activity were part and parcel of the life of faith, neither apart from it nor independent of it, and certainly not in conflict with it. Biblical faith had no room for anti-intellectualism; instead, faith and learning were mutually supportive and mutually enriching.

These examples illustrate the four emphases that were to shape higher education. The concern for moral character and faith development ("care of the soul") is obvious, along with the broad uses learning served. The unity of truth is apparent in the contributions of "secular" learning to the theocentric worldview of these individuals. The Mosaic law addressed sex and marriage, food and festivity, property and working conditions, social justice and political order. Solomon's wisdom extended to friendship, marriage and family, work and wealth, life's fulfillment and its frustrations, even old age and death. In Daniel's view of history, the destiny of nations was in the hands of God, the just judge of all the peoples of the world, and Paul insisted that, whatever we do in whatever station in life, it should be done heartily as an offering to the Lord. This all-inclusiveness results from broad education and a contemplative approach to life; it involves not just doing things or doing them thoughtlessly, but reflecting on how whatever we do in life relates to its creator and lord. It makes life and learning a continuous doxology of praise to God.

Of particular importance for education is the biblical concept of wisdom. The first nine chapters of Proverbs, for instance, appear to be intended as moral education for a son, while Job and Ecclesiastes ponder the vicissitudes of life. Wisdom in these books is not just a body of knowledge or even a depth of understanding, for it requires good judgment that embodies fundamental values inherent in the overall meaning and purpose of life. In ancient Israel, as in other ancient Near Eastern cultures, an understanding of wisdom arose that emphasized the order of nature and a right ordering of the moral life and the basic structures of society. God's wisdom could be seen in his creation, and it should guide lives. The wisdom of ancient Israel was thus God-centered, since "the fear of the Lord is the beginning of wisdom."

This wisdom was based more in natural than in special revelation, and in creation rather than in God's covenant of law or grace, although some like Solomon and Daniel were specially gifted by God. Occasionally, as in Proverbs 8, wisdom is personified as having existed from before the beginning of creation, and as speaking what is right and true. But wisdom based only on human experience and the observation of nature is not always reliable or sufficient. Psalm 19 declares that while the heavens speak of God's wisdom, his law speaks more directly and more powerfully; this was also Paul's theme in his letter to the Romans, when he appealed not only to the witness of nature but also to God's law and his grace. Both natural and special revelation are therefore needed. In the New Testament, moreover, "one greater than Solomon" arrived (Matt. 12:42), for God's wisdom became incarnate in Jesus Christ. Paul calls Christ "the power and the wisdom of God," in contrast to the power of eloquent rhetoric that some of the Greeks regarded as wisdom (1 Cor. 1:20-31). Solomon had said that "wisdom is better than jewels," while Paul adds that "all the treasures of wisdom and knowledge" are hidden "in Christ" (Col. 2:3).

The letter to the Colossians was written to a Gentile church in a Hellenistic city where the main purpose of education was to acquire wisdom, namely, the proven values and the understanding of nature passed on from generation to generation through the liberal arts. But Paul points also to a specially revealed wisdom, for the Christ who created everything in heaven and earth and sustains its order has now come to reconcile it all to himself, and in everything he will eventually be supreme (1:15-19). Wisdom and knowledge, including the liberal arts, are therefore the treasures they are because they are about *his* wisdom and work, and so are about *him*. He is, after all, the cosmic Christ, the Christ of the entire creation, including all its arts and sciences. Paul contrasts this philosophy with one rooted only in this-world beliefs (2:8). True wisdom requires a distinctively Christian worldview.

Related to this biblical concept of wisdom is the personified Logos with whom John's Gospel begins. John probably had in mind the Hebrew term *dabar,* usually translated "word" in the Old Testament, since his opening line "In the beginning was the Word" recalls the opening line of Genesis: "In the beginning God created the heavens and the earth . . . and God said. . . ." But in the Hellenic world, *logos* was used not only for a speech or explanation, but also for intelligible order, for reasoning or even wisdom, used therefore about both rhetoric and philosophy (literally, "love of wisdom"). As the creative Word, then, Christ is God's most powerful rhetoric, calling worlds into being and calling us to himself; but as the divine Wisdom he was in the beginning with God, ordering the creation, and, by his coming, full of both grace and truth, he enlightens our understanding. John had experienced this himself, as his Gospel recounts, for he had heard and seen and touched the living Logos (1 John 1:1-3). Moreover, like Paul, he predicts that the Logos will eventually have the last word about the creation (Rev. 19:11-13).

It is a short step, as we shall see, from the biblical concepts of wisdom and logos to a theological foundation for the four Christian emphases we noted in higher education. In addition to their implications for faith, for moral development, and for the unity of truth in a Christocentric worldview, they invite the student of arts and sciences to contemplate for himself the eternal wisdom of God, which made these disciplines and their usefulness possible in the first place.

TWO

The Alexandrian School
and the Unity of Truth

Christianity's engagement in higher education began in third-century Alexandria, where the extended studies that Clement and Origen introduced in the catechetical school provide a paradigm for Christian thinking about higher education, and particularly about the unity of truth wherever it is found, in secular or distinctively Christian learning. Alexandrian Christianity adapted for its own purposes not only Alexandria's particular academic emphases but also the broader pattern of Hellenic education underlying them. In order to understand both the Alexandrian school and subsequent Christian thinking about higher education, therefore, we must look at it in relation to the broader tradition of education in the Hellenic world at large.[1]

Alexandria was an important center of ancient learning. Ptol-

1. On ancient education, the classic sources are H. I. Marrou, *A History of Education in Antiquity* (New York: Sheed and Ward, 1956), and Werner Jaeger's *Paideia: The Ideals of Greek Culture*, translated by Gilbert Highet (3 vols., New York: Oxford Univ. Press, 1944). See also J. F. Dobson, *Ancient Education and Its Meaning to Us* (New York: Cooper Square Publishers, 1963).

emy had established there a famous Museum (literally, a home of the "Muses") with a huge library and extensive botanical and zoological gardens. While primarily a research center supporting both scientists and poets, it attracted students from afar. Alexandrian scholarship emphasized an empirical approach both to science and to the study of language and literature, and this affected Jewish and Christian scholars. The Septuagint translation of the Old Testament, for example, was the work of seventy-two Alexandrian Jewish scholars, and Origen learned his critical skills and his interpretive methods of handling biblical literature by studying there.

Alexandria's advanced studies were built on the current pattern of a broad general education, preparatory to the study of rhetoric and philosophy. This system had developed from the early Greek concern to nurture in youth the aristocratic virtues of their culture, virtues which by the fifth century B.C. had given way to more democratic ideals and which later still gave way to the humanistic values of the Hellenistic age. Greece, it is said, progressed from a warrior society to a scribe culture.

From early times, children were taught to recite epic poetry, especially Homer, because by imitating the words and deeds and thereby identifying with the feelings of warrior heroes they would come to internalize heroic virtues as their own. Since reading and writing became necessary for this as well as for practical functions, the teaching of "grammar" came to include the study of both literature and language. Homer was read in both Greek and Roman schools, along with Aeschylus, Sophocles, Euripedes, and others. Mythology and some history were added to the curriculum, and the mythical stories were given allegorical meanings that contributed to the moral goals of education. In the late fourth century A.D., in his *Confessions*, Augustine described his reactions to studying Homer as a child. For him, as for many earlier and later generations, the recitation of poetry, in addition

9

to debates and prepared speeches, became the stuff of which the study of rhetoric was made.

Moral objectives remained primary for a long time. Among wealthy Greeks and Romans, a boy's life and morals were often entrusted to the supervision of a worthy slave who accompanied him to school and wherever he went outside the home. This *paidagogos* was to mentor and advise the youth, criticizing and disciplining him as severely as was necessary, and was often far more influential than the "grammar" teacher, at least in terms of moral formation.

Greek education, however, introduced young people to more than the virtues exemplified in their cultural heritage. Gymnastics prepared them for the athletic contests that were important in Greek society, as well as for military service. Vocal and instrumental music enabled them to participate in religious and civic rituals and celebrations. In time, a complete education became known as *enkuklios paideia,* the circle of learning, a phrase that is anglicized in our word "encyclopedia." Aristotle called it "liberal" (*eleutheros*) learning to indicate an education for freemen rather than slaves, one that makes citizens, body and soul, fit for the exercise of virtue. For him, virtue (*arete*) meant an overall excellence, both moral and intellectual, that actualizes the human potential for a complete life in accordance with reason. Reading and writing are needed to function effectively, gymnastics infuses courage, and music provides relaxing intellectual enjoyment that, through the effect of its modes and rhythms on the emotions, "tunes the soul to virtues."[2]

The phrase "liberal arts" achieved widespread currency in Roman times. Seneca, for example, distinguished "liberal studies" worthy of a freeborn gentleman from studies aimed at earning money. While liberal studies cannot actually bestow virtue, he ar-

2. Aristotle, *Politics,* viii.

gued, they do prepare the soul for its reception. Language, poetry, and history themselves do not bridle the passions or strengthen courage, kindness, and self-restraint, but, much as grammar prepares a child for liberal studies, so liberal studies prepare one for wisdom. The love of wisdom (philosophy, in its literal sense) referred to natural philosophy that investigates the natural order, to moral philosophy that keeps the soul in order, and to rational philosophy that keeps falsehood from displacing truth.[3]

The liberal arts included seven studies: the three verbal arts of grammar, rhetoric, and dialectic (or logic), and the four mathematical disciplines of arithmetic, geometry, astronomy, and music. The former (the trivium) were the focus of a humanistic and rhetorical emphasis in education, while the latter (the quadrivium) reflected a more philosophical emphasis. Pythagoras, for instance, taught mathematics as intellectual training rather than for its practical uses, and Plato claimed it could turn the soul from the world of change toward eternal truth. For Plato, the essence of higher education was the disciplined pursuit of truth, while for rhetoricians it was the transmission of traditional beliefs and virtues.[4]

The roots of this distinction can be found in Athens in the fifth century B.C., when the emergence of democracy made the skills required for political leadership a necessary commodity, and a demand grew for rhetoric along with practical wisdom. The "Sophists" (literally "wise men") who met these demands generally taught classical rhetoric, with its emphasis on breadth of knowledge and the orderly arrangement of an argument.

3. Seneca, Epistle 88, "On Liberal and Vocational Studies," in *Seneca ad Lucilium, Epistulae Morales*, vol. II, Loeb Classical Library (Cambridge, Mass.: Harvard Univ. Press, 1917).

4. For an extended discussion of these two views and their subsequent history, see Bruce A. Kimball, *Orators and Philosophers: A History of the Idea of Liberal Education* (New York: Teachers College Press, 1986).

Some were less principled: Gorgias, for instance, emphasized a powerful delivery, calling speech a despot who could do anything in the service of those he taught, and Protagoras was a relativist who asserted that "man is the measure of all things."

This unprincipled pragmatism aroused Socrates' criticism: he exposed the Sophists' unthinking relativism and called attention back to moral virtues, insisting that virtues are not relative to success but are unchanging and universal ideals. Because he taught his students to pursue the truth for themselves with careful analytic thinking, Socrates was accused of corrupting the youth of Athens, but he responded that he sought only the improvement of the soul. Plato, his disciple, argued that moral and intellectual development must go hand in hand, and that the reasoned pursuit of truth is essential to good political leadership. For this reason the education Plato proposed in his *Republic* was aimed at developing the wisdom necessary for a just society or a just ruler. Literature must be rightly selected, argued Plato, and he criticized Homer for portraying the gods doing things which men are condemned for doing. The right kind of music could calm the passions and prepare the mind for mathematics and abstract thought, but dialectic, the logical scrutiny of ideas and basic assumptions, was the philosophical skill for which Plato strove: it takes us beyond the relativity of experience and opinion to what is universally and unchangeably true. Since liberal education prepares one for philosophy and philosophy is what equips one to rule, Plato thereby limited advanced education and political leadership to an elite few who could qualify both intellectually and morally.

Although a rhetorician, Isocrates largely agreed with Socrates' criticisms. Rhetorical trickery, ignorance of philosophy, and lack of concern for justice and truth contradicted the claim to teach wisdom. Some Sophist handbooks and rules of rhetoric reduced it to technique, whereas in reality, he argued, it requires native ability along with broad education and experience. Rhetoric is an art, and

12

like the art of war it must marshall all available materials and deploy them strategically to maximize one's advantage. Its power comes not from the rhetoric itself, but from the wisdom and example of the speaker, so Isocrates' own manuals were largely collections of his speeches that modeled what rhetoric could be.

A well-educated man, he said, must have the ability to deliberate and decide matters of all sorts, so he must listen to the poets, learn from the sages, associate with the wisest, and develop a well-equipped mind. Education, then, should include philosophy, but effective communication remains its culmination. The right word, says Isocrates, is the surest sign of good understanding. In fact, the ability to understand one another, and the power to persuade, to make ourselves clear to each other, and to discourse about what is true and just, are what elevate us above the beasts and make city-states, with their laws and their arts, possible. The art of discourse, *logos,* is what finally equips one for citizenship.

Isocrates has been called "the father of humanism." His educational goal of developing the whole person — intellectually, mentally, aesthetically, politically — captured fourth-century Greece and spread throughout the Hellenistic and Roman worlds, leading to the creation of a broadly educated, cultured people. Even Plato saw how this might be:

> It seems to me that his natural powers give him a superiority over anything that Lysis has achieved in literature, and also that in point of character he is of nobler composition; hence it would not surprise me if with advancing years he made all his literary predecessors look like very small fry. . . . For that mind of his contains an innate tincture of philosophy.[5]

5. Plato, *Phaedrus,* 279a (Hackforth trans.). For Isocrates himself, see *Isocrates,* 2 vols., trans. G. Norlin, Loeb Classical Library (New York: G. P. Putnam's Sons, 1928-29).

Isocrates' achievement was in wedding wisdom to eloquence while insisting on a thorough knowledge infused with traditional values. In the Roman republic rhetoric became oriented largely to law, but Isocrates' advice still prevailed. Cicero observed that while wisdom without eloquence does too little for the good of the state, eloquence without wisdom is never helpful. Like the Stoics, he regarded philosophy as a school for virtue, because it identifies laws of nature to which the moral life should conform. Quintilian agreed: rhetorical style does not give rhetorical power, for that requires knowledge of poetry, history, and philosophy as well. A great orator must be a good man, for then he will more often say what is true and will only plead good causes. But goodness depends in part on natural impulses and in part on philosophical (i.e., moral) education, since a thorough study of the workings of nature shows that the entire world is governed by providence, and good men must therefore play their part in governing the state.[6]

This is Stoic language: nature is governed by rationally accessible laws of nature, disseminated like seeds of reason (*logoi spermatikoi*) that give life an order to which virtue conforms. *Logos* as "reason" and "order" underlies the philosophical tradition in Hellenistic education, while *logos* as "word" or "discourse" underlies the rhetorical. The logos concept embodied a philosophy of education.

Greek education tended to focus on politics and Roman education on law, but in the empire at large religion was more important. Having lost political freedom, people settled for peace and order and found inner liberty in their religion.[7] In third-

6. See Cicero, *De Oratore* and *De Inventione;* Quintilian, *Institutio Oratoria,* X and XII.1-6.

7. See Werner Jaeger, *Early Christianity and Greek Paideia* (Cambridge: Belknap Press of Harvard Univ. Press, 1961), p. 124, note 7.

century Alexandria, gnosticism flourished, and both gnosticism and Judaism established their own schools. The Alexandrian Jewish scholar Philo, himself educated in the Greek fashion, had earlier argued for combining humanistic and rabbinical education in an allegorical treatment of the biblical story about Abraham and Hagar. When Abraham failed to have a child by Sarah, she gave him her Egyptian servant Hagar instead. As an Egyptian, Hagar represents the Hellenistic education Alexandrians enjoyed, but mated with Abraham she prepared the way for Sarah, representing the divine philosophy. Grammar develops the intellect, music calms the passions, geometry sows seeds of justice by teaching equality and proportion, rhetoric trains our powers of observation and welds thought to expression, while dialectic distinguishes truth from error. Of his own education, Philo said that he brought it all as a gift to his lawful wife, the divine philosophy.

Philo in fact believed that Plato's philosophy had much in common with his Jewish faith, and his allegorical method of interpretation elicited Platonic themes from the Scriptures. Plato's forms are God's thoughts. The form of the good is God's wisdom celebrated in Proverbs and the apocryphal Wisdom of Solomon. God's wisdom is the logos, and the logos is God's activity of creating and governing an ordered universe and of giving the Torah. It is then both the divine word and divine reason whose image we as rational beings bear. So if all human learning, both Greek and Jewish, is due to the logos, then Greek learning can indeed be mated to love of divine wisdom and the study of Scripture. This is an argument we find repeated by Alexandrian Christians.

It was quite common, therefore, for both Jews and Christians to attend pagan schools. Tertullian had objected to Christians teaching in such situations, because in teaching about gods and pagan festivals one seemed to countenance idolatry; but studying in pagan schools was a different matter, because students needed the intellectual discipline and did not need to agree with

15

all they read.[8] Basil of Caesarea, in his "Address to Young Men on Reading Greek Literature," urged them not to leave the entire guidance of their lives to heathen teachers, yet he declared that many Greek poets taught virtue and that philosophy's love of wisdom could free the soul from bodily passions and point us to the eternal. Gregory of Nazianzus agreed, and in a panegyric on Basil called him "an orator among orators and a philosopher among philosophers." Gregory himself was a master of classical rhetoric: his broad learning and oratorical skills served, it was said, like musical instruments in a symphonic presentation of Christian beliefs and virtues.

While Christians benefited from Hellenistic education, however, Christian instruction generally went no further than an extended catechetical instruction. Clement of Rome, writing to the Corinthian church shortly before 100 A.D., first used the term "Christian education." He spoke of "*paideia* in Christ," echoing the apostle's language about raising children in the "*paideia* of the Lord" (Eph. 6:4), about Scripture being given for "*paideia* in righteousness" (2 Tim. 3:16), or about the law as a *paidagogos,* the mentor who guides us to Christ (Gal. 3:24). In such a Christian paideia, faith development is added to the moral objectives of Greek education, and catechetical instruction is naturally included.

In intellectual centers like Alexandria, however, more was necessary if faith development was to keep pace with the intellectual development of those attending the pagan schools and if Christians were to address their pagan peers on an equal intellectual level. Clement of Alexandria wanted to bring all available learning into the service of Christ, and in his *Stromata* he treats all the arts and sciences as gifts of God. Poetry trains our sensibilities, rhetoric sensitizes us to expression and dialectic to logi-

8. Tertullian, *On Idolatry,* x.

cal reasoning, while philosophy teaches contemplation. The art of rhetoric can be injurious, he warned, unless it is conjoined with philosophy, "a river of words, a drop of sense." Those who give themselves altogether to it have fallen in love with Hagar the handmaid and neglect the mistress. But God gave philosophy to the Greeks as he gave the law to the Jews, as a *paidagogos* to bring them to Christ. Philosophy contributes to this process in three ways: in seeking and contemplating the truth, in requiring principled behavior, and in shaping good men. All learning is useful.

The Greeks had always regarded moral formation and "the improvement of the soul," as Socrates put it, as the primary function of education, and the church fathers agreed that the study of literature and philosophy helped this process along. They admired Stoic moral teaching, perhaps too much, for Clement and others took self-control to the full extent of Stoic apathy, a passionless life devoid of desire and elation. In his *Paidagogos* (an image he used repeatedly), Clement presented Christ as the mentor who improves the soul, healing its passions and training it for a life of virtue by example, exhortation, and persuasion. Christianity was the true *paideia,* fulfilling education's ethical purpose to a higher degree than ever before, because the incarnate Logos was God's wise and powerful rhetoric addressed to all.

Origen, Clement's successor, was appointed to the catechetical school when just eighteen. The son of Christian parents who provided him with a close knowledge of Scripture and a thorough encyclic education, he grew up both a devoted Christian and a cultured Greek, and then studied Hebrew and Greek philosophy while teaching at the catechetical school. Over the years, with his classical education in language and literature, he made immense contributions to biblical scholarship — exegetical studies, critical studies to determine the text, and apologetic writings that used an allegorical method to explain difficult texts. According to a panegyric by Gregory Thaumaturgus, who studied with him later in Caesarea, Origen taught the standard "preliminary" studies. Mathematics and astronomy produced wonder at "the sacred economy of the universe." He taught ethics, and confirmed his teaching by his own actions so as to impart a well-disciplined, steadfast, and religious spirit. He taught dialectic to discipline the intellect and to protect it against deception on any subject whatever, and he urged study of the Greek philosophers as lovers of virtue. But encyclic knowledge not only frees us to satisfy the understanding and "enjoy the sweets of intellect," it also enables us to explore and explain Scripture.

Origen's teaching resembled that of the *paidagogos*. As was often the case then, students met and sometimes lived in their teacher's home, so that he became a mentor and model of virtue. As a child Origen had learned Christian morality from the Bible, and in his biblical commentaries he regularly expounded the moral significance of a text. Although the Mosaic law and the gospel lead us further, we do learn from the poets and philosophers, because natural moral law such as the Stoics taught is God's unchanging law for all his creatures. A century before Origen, Justin Martyr had explained why Stoic moral teaching was so admirable and the poets and philosophers so profitable for Christians; it was because the seed of reason, the logos, is implanted in every race of people.

Thus, while human wisdom can educate the soul, divine wisdom is the ultimate end. To become a Christian scholar, Origen advised Gregory (later bishop of Caesarea) to

> take with you on the one hand those parts of the philosophy of the Greeks which are fit to serve as general or preparatory studies for Christianity. . . . The children of the philosophers speak of geometry and music and grammar and rhetoric and astronomy as being ancillary to philosophy; in

18

the same way we might speak of philosophy itself as ancillary to Christianity.[9]

Then he drew an analogy: just as the Israelites, upon their liberation from slavery, took from the Egyptians the riches they would need for the worship of God, so at our liberation from idolatry we as Christians can bring the riches of Hellenistic learning to the word and service of God.

A pattern of thought began emerging to explain the usefulness of liberal learning and the moral teaching of pagan writers. This was important, because there was a question to be answered: how could the insights of the Stoics and especially of Plato be explained if Plato and the Stoics had no knowledge of either Christ or the Hebrew Scriptures? Christians, after all, appreciated much in Plato — his recognition that God is hard to find, that a divine artificer orders everything for good, and that the human soul is separable from the body and so survives death, as well as his emphasis on love for the Good and on the virtues. How could Plato be so wise? Justin Martyr had asked the same question. He first conjectured that the Greeks might have read Moses or met some of the Old Testament prophets, but eventually concluded that in the human mind lies a seed of the divine Logos. The "Middle Platonism" of the first and second centuries identified the Stoic logos with a divine intelligence that

9. Origen, *Letter to Gregory* (bishop of Caesarea), i. Cp. *Contra Celsum*, VI. xiii-xiv; *De Principiis*, I.ii. Also J. W. Trigg, *Origen: The Bible and Philosophy in the Third Century Church* (Atlanta: J. Knox Press, 1983); S. R. C. Lilla, *Clement of Alexandria: A Study in Christian Platonism and Gnosticism* (London: Oxford Univ. Press, 1971); and C. A. Bigg, *Christian Platonists of Alexandria* (Oxford: Clarendon Press, 1886). A similar attitude to pagan literature developed in ancient Britain, where Saxon poetry fulfilled the role that Greek poetry served in Alexandria. See David Jeffrey, *People of the Book* (Grand Rapids: Eerdmans, 1996), ch. 4.

contained all of Plato's forms. Philo, too, had appealed to the logos. Clement and Origen picked up on this line of thought.

In his *Exhortation to the Greeks,* Clement says that the Logos created the world in harmonious order and made humans in his own rational image. He was both preexistent with God the Father, enlightening human minds and disciplining his chosen people in ways of righteousness, and incarnate as Jesus Christ, revealing the Father and guiding us to him. He is both the ideal *paidagogos* and the ideal philosopher, both the Way and the Truth. In his commentary on John's Gospel, Origen adds that the Logos not only is the source of reason in every rational creature but also was "in the beginning" with God, the creator and the giver of rational order in nature. He is thus (1) the source of all being and order, (2) the light of reason that leads us to truth, and (3) the guide to virtue. Both Origen and Clement have in mind the personified divine wisdom of Proverbs 8 and of the apocryphal *Wisdom of Solomon* — itself a product of first-century Alexandrian Judaism. This threefold Logos is not the impersonal rational law of the Stoic logos, nor Philo's impersonal unity of forms, but a fully personal being distinct from God the Father. So when science traces the order of nature it is tracing God's wisdom, and the art that beautifies our lives enriches us with his beauty. All truth is God's truth no matter where it is found. This ultimately is why liberal learning and philosophy can contribute to the unity of truth that Scripture implies. This is the theological basis of Christian higher education.

The gospel, in Clement's thinking, is the meeting point of two traditions, the Hebrew and the Greek. Their history is one because truth is one; there is one river of truth, although many streams run into it. The full fruit of the gospel is born neither of reason without revelation nor of revelation without reason, for the two have one source. Exhibiting the unity of truth, however, is no easy task, and Origen approached it by interpreting the Bible in three ways: literally, morally, and allegorically, in line with Greek literary interpretation. Instead of exploring conceptual affinities and differences between biblical and Hellenic thought, he read biblical narratives as allegorical accounts of philosophical truths. But he was right that if truth is ultimately one, then the task of the church is to regather the fragments and reunite them to the body of truth as a whole. That is the goal for education that is loyal to Christ, to exhibit the unity of truth, the ideal *gnosis*.

If, as the psalmist says, the heavens declare the glory of God and the order of day upon day utters speech (*logos*), then there is no culture where the Logos is not heard. So the scholar joins the heavens day upon day in worshipful wonder at the Creator. In the Alexandrian school moral and spiritual formation and the usefulness of liberal learning joined the unity of truth in an all-encompassing doxology to the God of creation.

THREE

Augustine:
The Foundations of Education

Augustine was born in Roman North Africa in 354 A.D., a hundred years after Origen's death, and died in 430 while the Vandals were ravishing his homeland. As the Roman Empire declined, however, he was laying the foundations of education that would shape medieval learning and influence the Christian academy for centuries thereafter. His own teaching and writings continue the four emphases we have noted, but he develops more fully than his predecessors the foundations of liberal learning in a theology of creation.

His early education, as he describes it in his *Confessions*, reflected the limited nature of Roman schooling at that time.[1] Mainly "grammar," it was oriented more to formal rhetoric than to broadly liberal learning or moral formation. Reading poetry meant reading it with expression, explaining the significance of every word, and criticizing both the poetic form and the content. Augustine admits this gave him the ability to read whatever was

---

1. See H. I. Marrou, *History of Education in Antiquity* (New York: Sheed and Ward, 1956), part III, ch. 5.

set before him and to write whatever he wished, but he deeply regretted not mastering Greek. He especially loved Vergil (who took the place that Homer had occupied in Greece), and he often taught Vergil's works later in life. He complains, nevertheless, about rote learning and the teaching of rhetoric as a set of rules. The quadrivium was largely neglected, for astronomy was typically taught for the sake of mythology rather than mathematics, and geometry for the intellectual discipline that good rhetoric requires. Even worse, there was no serious pursuit of truth, and the moral influence of pagan literature troubled him. Truth and goodness — these were emphases Augustine's education lacked, and as a teacher he set out to supply them.

In the Roman Empire the ideal of a fluent speaker had taken precedence over the earlier Greek ideal of a cultivated and humane man of action. The growth of imperial power limited the freedom of public debate that had called for breadth of thought and analytic thinking, so that rhetoric now required the student to develop the memory, to give close attention to every detail of language, and to feel and express the whole range of human emotions in entertaining "declamations." It could lead to a career in law or to prestigious political appointments, but in any case the professional rhetor was highly regarded and had entrée into cultured society. To become a rhetor, Augustine studied in Carthage, a city second only to Rome in that part of the empire. He was an unsophisticated country boy, and recalls that mispronouncing one word was deemed a greater sin than hating a fellow student. But he eventually rose to the top of his school and was filled with conceit over the acclaim his winning orations received. He began to study law, but found it was based on human conventions rather than on some underlying natural law or any unchanging law of God. Truth and goodness were still missing.

Pride was not his only moral problem. Rhetoric taught him to feel emotions and to express them in measured ways, but the emotions of this teenager in a big city were a tumultuous tangle. He loved the theater, discovering reflections of his own inner struggles in what he saw and heard, but it fueled his inner torment and he enjoyed the sexual excitement it aroused. In love with love, he took a concubine with whom he lived for the next fifteen years. How else could he bring measure and form to his disordered love?

Then he read Cicero, and that began to change his life. Rather than reducing rhetoric to a set of rules and ignoring the ethical dimensions of what was addressed, Cicero talked even more than Isocrates of an eloquent wisdom that combined rhetoric with philosophy. This was not the relentless questioning and arguments of some traditions but, rather, that love of the good which Plato had idealized. Rhetoric was in this way wedded to a broad cultural understanding and the quest for truth. Augustine's dreams of oratorical fame gave way to a passionate search for truth and goodness. He began reading systematically in the liberal arts, the quadrivium as well as the trivium in which he had been schooled, still admitting his ignorance of the real source of their truth. Although raised as a Christian, he thought Manicheism's materialism, with its dualism of good and evil forces, best explained the world in general and his own moral struggles in particular — until the leading Manichean apologist proved unable to answer his objections. For a while he then inclined to scepticism about all human knowledge, but from Plato he learned that if truth is unchanging it must also be immaterial, and this set him in a constructive direction.

He taught rhetoric in Carthage and then moved to Rome where the opportunities seemed greater — except that students too often failed to pay their teacher. Soon he won an appointment to Milan as the city's official rhetor. Milan was a cultural and intellectual center, a seat of the imperial court in the western part of the empire. There he was captivated by the eloquent wisdom of Bishop Ambrose, a former local governor with Ciceronic rhetoric and Platonic leanings, whose sermons helped Augustine see that, if truth and goodness are immaterial, then God is too. Augustine gave himself to studying the Scriptures, discovering there a higher wisdom than he had seen anywhere else and a love for God that would reorder his life. At the age of thirty-two he became a Christian.

Ever since Isocrates, the rhetorical tradition had recognized that we learn by talking through our ideas with others, and in Augustine's day Roman senators and other wealthy citizens would occasionally retire to their country estates to reflect and write.[2] This practice of the *otium liberale,* a cultural retreat and learning community, appealed to Augustine. He had a lot to think through, his teaching and other duties had taken a toll on his health, and he was offered a suitable place at Cassiciacum, so with a few friends and students he explored some of the basic questions that had troubled him and recorded these discussions in a series of books. One, *Against the Academicians,* contends that knowledge of unchanging truth is indeed possible. *On the Good Life* argues that true happiness lies in possessing the good rather than in endlessly pursuing it; that is to say, it lies in finding God, the Truth, and the wisdom that comes from him. Perhaps the most significant work for a philosophy of education, *On Order,* claims that the order of creation is the basis for all human knowledge. Lying awake at night, Augustine debated with himself about the soul's thirst for truth, recording those reflections as *Soliloquies.* He also planned to write a book on each of the seven liberal arts but succeeded in completing only part of one on music.

This kind of *otium liberale* proved so valuable that, when shortly he returned to his native Africa, he established a similar

2. Peter Brown, *Augustine of Hippo: A Biography* (Berkeley: Univ. of California Press, 1969), ch. 11.

Christian community in Hippo that became the precursor of medieval monastery schools. There he continued writing, but he was increasingly called upon to serve the local church, first as priest and then as bishop, until he became one of the major theologians of his day. His attention focused increasingly on theological and ecclesiastical issues, and he started writing about the usefulness of liberal learning in the study and teaching of Scripture. This task too was interrupted by other duties, but he eventually completed it just four years before his death. *On Christian Doctrine* would become enormously influential in church-related education throughout medieval and Reformation times.

Fundamental in all of this, however, was a question he asked himself in his *Soliloquies:* "What do you want to know?" His response went far beyond the utilitarian learning of that day to what is eternal; "God and the soul," he replied, "nothing else!" As the Westminster Shorter Catechism put it centuries later, our highest end is "to glorify God and enjoy him for ever." Augustine applied that ideal to education. If we think it too removed from liberal learning, we miss the meaning of a "highest good," which is not just the chief among many goods, but the all-inclusive good that gives every other good its value. So a doxological refrain pervades Augustine's *Confessions;* every good he experiences and all the truth he learns come ultimately from God and are occasions for praise. God is the being "by whom all things are true that are true, and all things are good that are good." Liberal learning leads to the contemplation of God, and, for Augustine and the medievals who followed his lead, it elicited an ongoing commentary of prayer and praise.[3]

To see how liberal learning leads to the contemplation of God, we must look at its foundations in Augustine's theology of cre-

---

3. Anselm's *Proslogium,* arguing for God's existence while simultaneously addresssing him, is a monastery abbot's studied contemplation.

ation. While in Carthage he had written a book that is no longer extant, *On Beauty and Proportion,* and at Cassiciacum he developed the same general theme on truth and goodness. All of creation is providentially ordered in harmonious ways, such that not even ugliness and evil fall outside the created order on which they prey. The liberal arts develop the mind's ability to see nature's laws and so to enjoy its order and beauty. Grammar reveals rules of language, dialectic shows the logical structure of thought, rhetoric teaches ways of moving emotions, while mathematics and astronomy find rational order throughout nature. *On Order* is explicit about all this, but Augustine's ideas are most fully worked out in *On Music,* in his discussion of this one specific discipline. Here he traces the mathematical structure of rhythm (he never finished an intended part on melody) to the "judicial numbers" by which its form is evaluated. He had intended the same sort of treatment for the other disciplines as well, to show that they too exemplify archetypal ideas *(rationes aeternae)* in the divine mind. Plato's influence is obvious here, but in a limited way, for the eternal forms are no longer independent entities but ideals conceived by the creator. Cicero's influence is present also; for Cicero the goal of liberal learning was wisdom, for Augustine it is the wisdom of God. Faith and liberal learning contribute to each other: the created order evident in the arts and sciences points to the mind of the creator, while believing in God enlarges and recasts that understanding. Faith is understanding's step and understanding is faith's reward.

We see here how secular learning can reveal timeless truth and grasp values that Christians embrace, for truth and goodness exist objectively as ideals in the mind of God that shape his creation. Plato was right about their objectivity, even though he did not see their source in the divine Logos, as Augustine does. Augustine argues that philosophy has three branches:[4] natural phi-

---

4. Augustine, *City of God,* VIII.

losophy, in which God is the source of all being; rational philoso-phy, in which he is the source of all knowledge and truth; and moral philosophy, in which he is the source of all that is good. These three correspond to the threefold Logos in Clement's and Origen's work: the Logos of creation, of reason, and of salvation.

The soul and knowing God go together: "God in his ineffable way has used the mutable creation, obedient to his eternal laws, to remind the soul of its original and perfect nature."[5] Augustine knew, however, that his own disordered soul affected his pursuit of wisdom, and that nothing hinders wisdom more than a life de-voted to earthly pleasure, fame, or power. Writing to a former fellow-student he had led into Manicheism, he recalled their teenage attitude to the Scriptures.

> But we, intelligent youths, marvelous explorers of reason, without turning over these books and without seeking teach-ers, without the slightest suspicion of our own slowness of comprehension, without the slightest heed paid to those whose care it had been that these books be read, guarded, and studied throughout the world and for so long a time — we had the temerity to suppose that nothing such men said was to be believed.[6]

On Order thus insists that studying the divine wisdom requires a right ordering of the soul as well as of the studies themselves. Au-gustine warns about a life devoted to pleasure, about indolence and sluggish minds, about jealousy, hate, and anger, and about despair of ever finding the truth. In a more constructive vein he identifies seven stages in the improvement of one's soul: (1) fear of God will counter the pride that makes a student unteachable and

5. Augustine, *On True Religion*, xix.
6. Augustine, *The Usefulness of Belief*, xiii; *On True Religion*, iii.

will lead to (2) a piety toward God that instills (3) hope, so that (4) knowledge of Scripture can engender (5) love for both God and neighbor (6) and cleanse the mind to see (7) God's wisdom.[7]

Mere curiosity will not help. The curious, he says, ask about things they do not really care about, because they have no real love of wisdom. The Athenian philosophers in Acts 17 were interested only in novel ideas, while others engage in pointless speculations, taking delight in the game of learning rather than in actually knowing the truth. The studious, on the other hand, ask about things that really concern them, things that contribute to liberal education and the equipping of their souls. They really love wisdom. Curiosity and studiousness are two different kinds of love, the one *(cupiditas)* ill-directed toward lesser and more fleeting ends, the other *(charitas)* well-ordered toward truth and goodness.[8] For the studious who really want to contemplate God's wisdom, *On Order* proposes a fourfold path. They must first see the wisdom in regulating their lives, then explore reason, the image of God in us, then consider the "Intelligence" that unites the entire creation order, and thus contemplate its source in the wisdom of God.

This order involves both authority and reason. Developmentally authority comes first, as in teaching young children or the regulation of student life. In reality, however, reason always comes first, whether from the divine wisdom that governs the creation or the human wisdom of teachers. Only God's authority is absolute. Human authorities may tell us what to believe or how to act but, since they are sometimes mistaken or deceive us, rational beings need to consider whom and what to believe, and

7. Augustine, *The Measure of the Soul,* xxxiii-xxxvi.

8. Augustine, *The Usefulness of Belief,* elaborates on this distinction which underlay the medievals' rejection of mere curiosity.

then ascribe the highest authority to what is most clearly known. Authority naturally prepares us for reason.

As rational beings we plan actions with specific ends in mind, we use language to distinguish or connect things in orderly ways, we contemplate the rhythm of a piece of music or the architectural design of a building. In all of this, reason moves beyond sense experience to forms that we grasp with the mind. The trivium develops this capacity in disciplined ways. Dialectic does so by analyzing definitions to eliminate what is irrelevant and by synthesizing similarities to form general concepts. Grammar studies the structure and power of language, while rhetoric teaches debaters to get to the heart of an issue, organize arguments, and stick to the point. The disciplined, well-ordered mind is better equipped to grasp the truth.

We discover the truth and contemplate it not *in* the senses but *through* them. In the quadrivium (arithmetic, geometry, astronomy, and music), we grasp the underlying order by abstracting it from particulars, like the concept "3" apart from the three sides of any triangle, or a triangle apart from the spacing of any three heavenly bodies. The properties of numbers and triangles are independently and unchangeably true, and they draw the mind away from the external world of the senses to what is seen only within the mind. It is there that reason begins to understand the wisdom with which God governs his creation.

As rational beings, then, we think abstractly. Augustine argues in *On the Teacher* that a teacher's words and the things we read, like other sense objects, do not themselves reveal the truth but simply alert the mind to think about an inherent order of things by the inner light of reason with which God illumines the mind. The real teacher is the one who teaches within the soul, namely the divine Logos. Plato had maintained that dialectic by itself enables the mind to recollect eternal forms, but Augustine replaces Plato's recollection with divine illumination, a general enlightenment of human reason that enables it to grasp the universal forms by which God orders his creation. It is the divine Logos himself who enables human reason to contemplate the wisdom of God.

A person is given only as much light as he or she is able to receive, relative to the moral disposition of the will, and so the educator must pursue moral as well as intellectual development. Augustine breaks with Cicero in declaring that we are not ruled by what we know but by what we love. Philosophy was, after all, the *love* of wisdom. He begins *On Christian Doctrine* by proposing that some things are to be enjoyed, others used, and others both enjoyed and used. We enjoy something when we cling to it with love, for its own sake, while we use it to obtain some other thing that we love. Liberal learning may have all sorts of uses, depending on what we love, but it may also be enjoyed; and it serves our highest love when it leads to the contemplation of God.

Augustine therefore points beyond reason's perception of creation's many intelligible forms to the overall unity of truth in the divine intelligence. His language is borrowed from the Neoplatonists (for whom Intelligence was the highest emanation from the eternal One), but his own intention is clear: this divine intelligence is in reality the wisdom of God, the eternal Logos who became incarnate for our salvation.

On Christian Doctrine exemplifies the way in which liberal learning can be both enjoyed for its own sake and used for some other end, for it discusses how the liberal arts he so plainly enjoyed should be used in the study and teaching of Scripture. That should of course be a labor of love but, like everything else in creation, love must be properly ordered, directed toward God and neighbors as well as one's own soul. So to study Scripture aright the soul must be freed from the disorder of lower desires: moral and intellectual development are both required.

Augustine also reaffirms his appreciation for pagan learning.

31

Philosophers in general, and "especially the Platonists," have said things that are true and agree with the Scriptures and that can accordingly be converted to Christian use. Moses was instructed in the wisdom of the Egyptians (Acts 7:22), and when the Israelites fled they took with them Egyptian treasures that had originally been dug from "mines of divine providence." Of course these were little compared with the treasures which the wisdom of Solomon later provided, and so too is all the treasure we gather from pagan books compared with holy Scripture.[9] But all truth is ultimately the wisdom of God, and it was made accessible to human reason by the light of the Logos, no matter where it is found.

Augustine wants to bring to Scripture the kind of close and detailed exposition to which he was exposed in his own education and which he subsequently taught, but wants to do so with input from the whole breadth of liberal learning. Scripture must not be read superficially, but with reason searching for the underlying order, possibly an order that only the divine author who guided the writer knew. Augustine therefore stresses the complex uses of language, then moves to examples from music and history, natural science and geography, dialectic and rhetoric, and arithmetic and philosophy that shed light on the interpretation of biblical texts.

Finally, he addresses the art of teaching, and here he draws on his own discipline of rhetoric. Like Cicero, his professional model, and Isocrates before him, he declines to focus on formal rules but advises would-be teachers to listen to or read model speeches, and to practice writing and dictating speeches as well as delivering them. Show that what you say is reasonable, he advises, but avoid fancy or frothy language, for good minds love the truth within the words rather than the words themselves. The ideal is eloquent wisdom, that is, divine wisdom based on an

9. Augustine, *On Christian Doctrine,* II.xl-xliii.

understanding of Scripture informed by the liberal arts, with an eloquence true to Cicero's saying that "to teach is a necessity, to please is sweetness, to persuade is victory." When you urge students to do something, Augustine says, teach so as to instruct (for understanding the truth is a necessity), please so as to hold attention, and persuade so as to win assent. Even so, a teacher's consistent life will still carry greater weight than any eloquence.

Augustine also addresses the issues of teaching and rhetoric in a short piece entitled *On Catechizing the Uninstructed*. Liberally educated catechumens with a knowledge of literature and science will appreciate teaching that helps them think through what is on their minds, he writes, but one must never talk down to those less educated. Keep the rhetoric simple, so that they can listen for the truth rather than be mesmerized by words or by pleasing but superficial ideas. Teaching, like learning, must reach beyond what people see and hear to lasting truth that instructs and forms the soul.

Augustine remained in the Hippo community he had founded, and he continued writing to the end of his days: letters and sermons, biblical studies, treatises on theological and ecclesiastical matters, and discussions of moral and social issues. His voice, for instance, was crucial in the Pelagian controversy over sin and grace, an issue on which he remained for centuries the most significant teacher of the entire church. When in 410 the Goths sacked Rome and many attributed it to her forsaking the pagan gods, he spent thirteen years writing his *magnum opus, The City of God*; it was a theological reading of human history as a tale of two cities with two loves, the one loving God in and above all else, the other loving with that kind of debased and disordered love from which he himself had been saved. His theological foundations of education had become theological foundations for Rome itself and for all of human history.

FOUR

Monastery and Cathedral Schools:
The Care of the Soul

As Rome declined under barbarian invasions, Roman education disintegrated and libraries were often gutted. The revival of learning took centuries, but throughout that process Augustine's *On Christian Doctrine* remained a major influence. In the sixth century, Boethius helped preserve Greek learning by translating parts of Aristotle's *Organon* into Latin and writing various commentaries, so that until the twelfth century scholars owed to him all they knew not only of Aristotle and his logic but also of much of the quadrivium. The logic was incomplete and largely dialectic with its emphasis on defining essences, making distinctions, and following a logical order, all of which are useful in expounding texts. It was Boethius, moreover, who distinguished several questions about essences that would shape the medieval debate about universals. Like Augustine, he found order everywhere. He saw the cosmic music of the spheres, for example, as matched not only by the music of instrumentalists and poets but also by the "human music" that harmonizes various parts of the soul with each other and with the body. Nothing is more characteristic of human nature than to be soothed by pleasant modes of music and disturbed by their opposite, so that radical transformations of character also arise.[1] Not only music but all the quadrivium teaches moral wisdom as well as the archetypal wisdom of the creator, and so the Middle Ages viewed liberal learning as contributing both to biblical interpretation and to moral development, and increasingly to spiritual formation and the contemplation of God.

A student of Boethius who became a Roman senator, Cassiodorus, followed Augustine's example in establishing a school where priests could learn what they needed of the liberal arts to study and teach the Scriptures in an intelligent fashion. The liberal arts, he believed, were the seven pillars of wisdom (Prov. 9:1) and the seven lamps that illumined the tabernacle (Exod. 25:37), so his *Institutiones*[2] introduced the contents first of Scripture and then of the seven liberal arts, emphasizing the task of expounding and correcting these texts. His school later developed into a monastery with a scriptorium where copies of classical and biblical texts were made which contributed to the renewal of learning. In the meantime, however, care of the soul remained an immediate goal. Arithmetic sharpens the mind for contemplation, drawing it away from carnal desires to the desire for wisdom. And music that calms the emotions raises the mind to heavenly things: the heart's beating shows by its musical flow if it is in accord with virtue.

It was Charlemagne who initiated the widespread development of monastery and cathedral schools. Impressed by the contributions of Irish monks, he first brought Alcuin from one of their recently established monasteries in Britain to start a palace

---

1. Boethius, *De Institutione Musica,* clxxx, trans. Calvin M. Bower (New Haven: Yale Univ. Press, 1989), p. 2.

2. Cassiodorus, *An Introduction to Divine and Human Readings,* trans. L. W. Jones (New York: Octagon Books, 1966).

school, then appealed to bishops and abbots to develop schools that would teach "the highest wisdom" through the study of Scripture and the liberal arts.

The monastery schools prepared monks for the contemplative life and took students from outside the cloister only occasionally. They therefore emphasized moral and spiritual formation, focusing primarily on the affections and desires; one classical study of monastic culture, for instance, is entitled *The Love of Learning and the Desire for God*.[3] This was humanistic learning based on classical literature, and some of the monks who appreciated the beauty and excellence of Latin style wrote fine poetry themselves. They had mixed reactions to the content of classical literature, as had Augustine and the patristic writers, but they still found wisdom in particular episodes, characters, and insightful sayings. Their contemplation was enriched by allegorical interpretations, for they saw the universe not only as an orderly unity that displayed God's wisdom and power but also as an elaborate system of symbols and signs of spiritual truth. They read not passively but actively, pronouncing each word pensively with their lips so as to assimilate its meaning, and they read in a liturgical context under the direction of the abbot, who guided their moral and spiritual formation.

The cathedral schools, on the other hand, were usually located at episcopal seats, hence in cities, and generally prepared people with some prior education in the liberal arts for further studies in theology or law, and for the active life of pastors and administrators in church or civil society rather than for the contemplative life of a monk. Their focus accordingly became "letters and manners," "letters" being the liberal arts with special at-

3. Jean Leclercq, *The Love of Learning and the Desire for God: A Study of Monastic Culture,* trans. Catherine Misrahi (New York: Fordham Univ. Press, 1961).

tention to the trivium, and "manners" the virtues expected of such leaders, like moderation, humility, and patience. Letters produce eloquence, manners produce practical wisdom — hence the now traditional objective of "eloquent wisdom."[4]

Ideally, the most formative influence was not the content of instruction but the charismatic teacher. Bernard of Clairvaux, for example, was praised for "a miraculous exercise of teaching through his physical presence."[5] Students learned by "reading" their teacher — his character, habits, and attitudes as well as his words and deeds. Like the Greek *paidagogos,* he was the moral authority, a model, exemplar, and disciplinarian; his graces made Jesus Christ seem physically present. He molded the student with discipline, it was said, as a potter molds clay at his potter's wheel, and, since he maintained an ongoing conversation with each of his students, they developed a friendship in which each grew to love and admire the virtues in the other.

Cathedral schools absorbed an overflow of students from palace schools, and in time the growing luxury and avarice of court life filtered down as well. Perhaps the arrogance of wealth encouraged an arrogance of intellect, but, whatever the reason, argumentative students began to challenge the authority and discredit the thinking of their teachers. Such was the plight of William of Champeaux early in the twelfth century at Notre Dame cathedral in Paris, when a brilliant student named Abelard, whose unrelenting dialectic would later become notorious, forced him to change his view about universals. With some of his other students, William left Notre Dame for a more contemplative environment in the abbey at St. Victor, on the outskirts of the city but near

4. See C. Stephen Jaeger, *The Envy of Angels: Cathedral Schools and Social Ideals in Medieval Europe, 950-1200* (Philadelphia: Univ. of Pennsylvania Press, 1994).

5. Jaeger, *The Envy of Angels,* p. 80.

enough to keep in touch with its intellectual life. When he later left the abbey to become a bishop, the new school's influence grew under the articulate and charismatic teaching of Hugh of St. Victor.

The school at St. Victor was an "open" school in two regards, open to students from outside the abbey and open to ideas from other schools in the area. It maintained a serious intellectual life while avoiding the argumentativeness that had developed at the cathedral, and "letters and manners" continued to be stressed. Faced with the intellectual and moral problems of human nature, Hugh wanted to provide curatives that would help restore both the rational image of God and humanity's moral likeness to him. God dwells in us by knowledge and love, so letters and manners would teach students to understand the truth and to know the good — truth and good being the two parts of wisdom. To know God is to love him, Hugh declared, and nobody loves him without knowing him, for God is both the Truth and the Good. In this fashion the Victorines sum up the influence that Augustine's *On Christian Doctrine* had on education during the previous seven hundred years.

Hugh's *Didascalicon,* written in the 1120s, told his students what they should read to implement these goals and how they should read it. While nothing they studied would ever be superfluous if they developed the right study habits, they would need an aptitude to gather knowledge and the memory to retain it. Three steps were involved. Natural aptitudes would be developed by thinking (*cogitatio*) as one read, and disciplined by basing interpretations on a careful study of words and grammar. Simply being aware of the ideas and images that came to mind was not enough, for texts had to be expounded by defining and analyzing every aspect of the language. Meditation (*meditatio*) then had to reexamine all the ideas to get at the truth involved, scrutinizing the virtues and vices and pondering what it all said about the wisdom and goodness of God. Beyond thinking and meditation came *contemplatio,* the delight of contemplating the overall picture and seeing hidden meanings that eventually came to light. Hugh illustrated these later stages of learning, describing Proverbs as a meditation on the moral dimensions of life, Ecclesiastes as a contemplation of the overall human condition, and the Song of Solomon as a loving contemplation of the coming of our Bridegroom, Jesus Christ.

Hugh's curriculum addressed the same goals and included writings of the church fathers as well as the seven liberal arts and the Scriptures. The theoretical arts (the quadrivium and theology) remedied ignorance of the good, practical arts taught practical wisdom about the moral and civil life, the mechanical arts (agriculture and medicine) sustained life, while logic grasped the ordered unity of creation and the unity of all truth in the mind of God.

> The human mind, stupefied by bodily sensations and enticed out of itself by sensuous forms, had forgotten what it was and, because it does not remember that it was anything different, it believes it is nothing but what is seen. But we are restored by instruction, so that we may recognize our true nature and learn not to seek outside ourselves what we can find within. The highest curative of life, therefore, is the pursuit of wisdom.[6]

That he has in mind divine as well as human wisdom is evident, for he adds that while in human minds the idea of a human body images the human being, in God's mind the human being images an eternal ideal, his archetype of what it really is to be human. Thus contemplation that sees truly the essence of human nature

6. Hugh of St. Victor, *Didascalicon: A Medieval Guide to the Arts,* trans. Jerome Taylor (New York: Columbia Univ. Press, 1961), p. 47.

or of any other created thing knows something of the wisdom of God: so Augustine's Logos doctrine remained the theological foundation for human learning.

But Hugh taught another way of seeing God in creation, a way other than contemplating essences. Like most medievals, he held a sacramental view of the universe, such that visible things have attributes analogous to their invisible cause and the overall hierarchy of being therefore reveals the divine presence. Contemplation in the quadrivium thus produced a symbolic reading of nature. In mathematics a number like three had religious significance, as light did in astronomy and harmony in music, for all of nature bespeaks the inner presence of God. Hugh, of course, followed a long tradition in this use of symbolism, one that guided reading in the liberal arts and Augustine's interpretation of Scripture.

> All the arts of the natural world subserve our knowledge of God, and the lower wisdom leads to the higher. The trivium serves the literal meaning, the quadrivium the figurative meaning. Above and before all these is that divine being to whom Scripture leads by faith and works; in the knowledge of whose truth and the love of whose excellence man is restored to his true nature.[7]

In addition to the symbolic or allegorical, Hugh, more than many of his contemporaries, stressed a literal or historical reading of Scripture and its tropological or moral significance. In dis-

---

7. Hugh of St. Victor, quoted by Margaret Gibson in "'De Doctrina Christiana' in the School of St. Victor," in *Reading and Wisdom: The De Doctrina Christiana of Augustine in the Middle Ages,* ed. Edward English (Notre Dame, Ind.: Univ. of Notre Dame Press, 1995), p. 43. On medieval symbolism and its assumptions about the referential nature of the created world, see David Jeffrey, *People of the Book* (Grand Rapids: Eerdmans, 1996), ch. 5.

cussing Noah's ark, for instance, he writes of the literally wooden vessel Noah made as well as the figurative ark Christ made when he gathered the nations into a saving faith; in addition, wisdom builds the moral ark in our hearts through knowledge and love, uniting the many virtues into one love for God. "Set charity in order," he echoes Augustine again, "that desire may run from God, with God, to God."[8]

Quintilian had advised that "morals equip learning." For this reason also moral formation was an essential part of the contemplative life. The study of Scripture provided examples and advice about developing virtues and avoiding vices, but most of all it fed good desires and inflamed the mind with love for God. Hugh cautioned against reading the Bible carelessly, omitting what ought to be learned or failing to think beyond the words to their moral significance. Moral development requires a humility that is eager to learn from whatever source, a quiet life undistracted by illicit desires or undue business, and a simple life free from needless cravings — so he added rules for living to his rules for study. Silence was required at meals, so they could listen thoughtfully to readings from Augustine's homilies or commentaries. Because the visible signifies the invisible, he required modesty in dress and eating and forbade courtly manners such as a swagger, a "wanton strut," or an "effeminate glide." Bernard of Clairvaux had said that moral growth begins in the conscience, not the body, but Hugh was concerned about both, for, while virtue is indeed a habit of the heart, it is acquired, as Aristotle had taught, by acting habitually on considered decisions to do what is right.

By the thirteenth century, university learning was becoming more narrowly academic. With the rediscovery of Aristotle's nat-

---

8. *Hugh of St. Victor: Selected Spiritual Writings*, trans. by a religious of C.S.M.V., Intro. by Alfred Squire (New York: Harper and Row, 1962).

ural science and his remaining logical works, syllogistic proofs were now expected and Abelard's disputational approach became almost the norm. The Victorines, however, had preserved the Augustinian approach, which Bonaventure would now develop more systematically while scholasticism was at its height in Paris. After early schooling in a Franciscan friary, Bonaventure had studied the liberal arts at the University of Paris in preparation for advanced work in theology. Entering the Franciscan order, he taught for a while in the university until, in 1257, he was chosen to head the order. So far-reaching were his contributions over the next seventeen years that he became known as the order's "second founder."

Francis of Assisi, its original founder, had preached brotherly love and peace, but a rift had developed over continuing the practice of poverty. Bonaventure refused to take sides, but made the good features of both the basis for restoring unity. Later in life he moderated a dispute over papal election and attempted to reunite the Greek and Roman churches. Such was his practice of the Franciscan ideal, and his concern for moral formation is evident in a brief book he wrote for heads of religious communities about how to get a community to live up to its ideals. Entitled *The Six Wings of the Seraphim*[9] (seraphim being the vanguard of the angelic host), it discusses six essential virtues of the servant-leader: zeal for righteousness, brotherly love, patience, an exemplary life, wisdom, and devotion to God.

Francis himself supposedly thought liberal learning needless except as it could be helpful in interpreting Scripture, and even dangerously prideful without the illumination that comes from Scripture, but he thought of nature as the mirror of God and as

---

9. See *The Character of a Christian Leader: Originally Titled The Six Wings of the Seraph by St. Bonaventure*, trans. Philip O'Mara (Ann Arbor: Servant Books, 1978).

providing steps to God. Bonaventure picked up these images, for he had to translate Francis's vision into a body of doctrine that could be taught and preached. For this reason he advocated a contemplative approach to liberal learning that would nourish the spiritual life while preparing priests and lay brothers for the study of theology. Grammar was for expressing the truth of Scripture, rhetoric for persuading belief in that truth, and logic for judging truth and falsity, while in natural philosophy a God-given light would reveal the divine cause of all that exists. The liberal arts could in this way nurture a love for God as the source of life and wisdom.

Despite his more positive view of the liberal arts, Bonaventure was not insensitive to Francis's concerns. The human mind is finite and fallen, handicapped by ignorance and concupiscence — what Augustine called disordered and misdirected love — so that by ourselves we can neither know nor love the good. Logic alone cannot prove the existence either of God or of the archetypal truths in his mind, and so there can be no natural theology or satisfactory philosophy unless the divine Logos enlightens the mind. The key to effective learning was therefore for Bonaventure, as it was for Augustine, a properly ordered and directed love. Do not assume, he urged, "that mere reading will suffice without fervor, speculation without devotion, investigation without admiration, observation without exaltation, industry without piety, knowledge without love, understanding without humility, study without divine grace."[10] There are moral and spiritual prerequisites for acquiring wisdom.

But wisdom is written everywhere, Bonaventure insists, and the world is like a book written front and back, or a mirror imag-

---

10. Bonaventure, *The Journey of the Mind to God*, trans. P. Boehner, with Introduction and notes by Stephen F. Brown (Indianapolis: Hackett Publ. Co., 1993), p. 2.

ing the presence of God in its order and beauty and light. A rose is not just a rose when it exists to praise its maker. God's goodness emanates like light diffusing itself throughout the entire creation; he is the exemplar, the Logos of all created things, and he is the one to whom it leads and for whom it all exists. Emanation, exemplarism, and consummation: these are the themes that shaped Bonaventure's worldview and thence his approach to learning.[11] They are all three Christocentric themes, for Christ is the Light of the world, the eternal Logos, and the object of contemplation and love.

Theology is the integrative discipline that reveals the unity of truth, but in explaining the connection of the arts to theology Bonaventure makes extended use of the image of light. The laws of nature are lights given by God to enlighten everyone who comes into the world. The light of the Logos is the ultimate natural form of every created thing, so different degrees of light, various kinds of light, and analogies and symbols for light are everywhere to be found. In his brief treatise, *On the Reduction of the Arts to Theology*,[12] he distinguishes the external light of the mechanical arts that gives structure to artifacts, the lower light of sense perception that recognizes natural forms, the inner light of reason that grasps eternal forms, and the higher light of sacred Scripture that reveals saving truth. That higher light produces a threefold interpretation of Scripture in addition to its literal meaning: the allegorical or symbolic, the moral, and the anagogical that points to a mystical union with God.

His classic introduction to the liberal arts, *The Journey of the Mind to God*, therefore does not follow the scholastic road of argu-

11. See Matt Benedictus, *The Social Thought of Saint Bonaventure* (Washington, D.C.: Catholic Univ. of America, 1946), ch. 2.

12. *Saint Bonaventure's De Reductione Artium ad Theologiam*, trans. E. T. Healy (St. Bonaventure, N.Y.: The Franciscan University, Saint Bonaventure Univ., 1955).

ment or conceptual analysis, but the way of faith seeking understanding, and in it all seeking God. It adopts Hugh of St. Victor's
cogitatio, meditatio, and *contemplatio,* as the mind moves from
things outside itself to things within itself, and then looks above.
Bonaventure starts with the visible world, the world of the quadrivium. In the overall hierarchy of beings, with its degrees of all
essential properties, the general properties of created things point
to God: that heavy objects fall suggests that all things tend toward
their proper end, which is God, while their limited size suggests
he is unlimited. The whole natural order points to limitless wisdom, goodness, and power. But Bonaventure is not content with
pointers to one beyond our experience, for he sees "vestiges" of
God's presence in his creatures. God is eternal Truth, and vestiges
of this are evident in our knowledge of archetypal ideas. God is
eternal Beauty, and the beauties that delight us here are vestiges of
that. He is eternal Light, and while every creature is by its very nature a likeness of eternal wisdom, some have also "the character of
sacrament" by virtue of God's presence.[13] Bonaventure finds in
the experience of truth and beauty through liberal learning something analogous to experiencing God in the sacrament.

From the external world of the quadrivium Bonaventure moves
to the natural powers within the soul itself, which like Augustine he
finds analogous to the divine trinity. *Memory* images the eternal Father by holding the past in present thought, the *intellect* grasps eternal Truth by illumination of the Logos, while *desire* leads the soul to
its highest good. This trinity of powers in the soul is enlightened by
liberal learning. Natural science's search for causes contemplates
the Father's power as creator; rational philosophy — the trivium of
grammar, logic and rhetoric — speaks of the wisdom and Logos of
God; and moral philosophy reveals his goodness. Liberal learning,
enlightened by the Logos, assists the soul's journey to God.

13. Bonaventure, *Journey of the Mind,* p. 16.

Bonaventure well knew that his students were prone to wander from this path, for he observed that memory becomes distracted by cares, intelligence confused by a multiplicity of changing experiences, and the desire for God drawn to lesser loves. This disorder can only be reformed when the presence of God in the soul imparts a trinity of virtues: faith in the eternal Word, hope that heeds the inspired Word, and love that delights in the Word incarnate. These theological virtues show how Christ the divine Logos can be present in the soul.

The final stage of the soul's journey leads the student from the liberal arts to theology and so to God himself. Here the initial step is a remaining area of natural philosophy, metaphysics, where God is understood as Being itself, the highest Good. Then contemplation rises beyond its intellectual labors to focus in loving adoration on a man who is God's perfect image, the ascended Christ. What is the process or method involved? Says Bonaventure, "Ask grace, not learning; desire, not understanding; prayer, not diligence in reading; the Bridegroom, not the teacher; God, not man."[14] It is a supremely doxological experience, the consummation of a Christian's path through liberal learning to God.

The medievals' symbolic reading of nature and their allegorical interpretation of Scripture seem strange to the contemporary mind, because we no longer see any hierarchy with underlying analogies between different kinds of beings. But if Bonaventure was right that God is present and active in nature and the human soul, then the love of learning and a desire for God can be one. If the heavens declare his glory, learning should still nurture faith and virtue, and lead to a contemplative delight in his presence.

14. Bonaventure, *Journey of the Mind*, p. 32.

FIVE

The Scholastic University:
Theology and the Liberal Arts

For most of the Middle Ages, education was almost entirely the church's province; it remained so until scholars like Abelard (d. 1142) began to pursue learning and teaching on their own, independently of the monastery and cathedral schools. Independent guilds of scholars developed in places like Paris, banding together to further their professional interests. Their students were like apprentices in craftsmen's guilds, learning and sometimes practicing the teacher's craft under the supervision of their masters until they themselves were credentialed as masters. Universities were made up of such guilds, with masters of the arts preparing students for teaching or for further studies in the faculties of theology, law, or medicine, so that in Paris most of the theology students were already masters of arts.

The thirteenth-century university was an intellectually exciting place, where previous uses of the liberal arts were being challenged by new teaching methods, previous explanations of the unity of truth by new ideas, and Christians themselves by a growing presence of Islamic thought. Liberal arts teaching had long focused primarily on the trivium, with detailed expository lectures on certain works of classical literature or the church fathers, supplemented by an examination of questionable interpretations.[1] The grammarian's concern for interpretation (literal, moral, and allegorical) had predominated, aided by the rhetorician's attention to oratorical devices and their emotional influence and by dialectic's close scrutiny of meanings and disputations about alternative views.

Abelard was particularly adept at dialectic, and particularly controversial as well, for he developed new dialectical techniques which, combined with his argumentative disposition and novel theological views, aroused the ire of traditional and pious clerics and scholars. Teaching authoritative texts was intended to elicit a stable body of knowledge, but he seemed to create more problems than he settled. Moreover, he rejected the Platonic and Augustinian view of universals as eternal exemplars in God's mind and ordering principles in the particulars of creation, accepting them only as abstract concepts. The analogy between God and his creation on which the traditional symbolic interpretation of nature depended was therefore groundless, and the contemplation of universal forms was not the way to contemplate God. Abelard preferred to get his theology directly from Scripture, so in *Sic et Non* he compiled quotations from biblical and patristic writers both in favor of and against the use of traditional doctrines as source material for dialectical disputations. He also criticized the rules by which religious orders like the Victorines attempted to shape character, arguing that sin is basically an inner consent to evil rather than overt behavior. For these reasons he was accused of lacking concern for the moral and spiritual development of his students, of trying to clarify mysteries of faith that were intended

1. Hastings Rashdall, *The Universities of Europe in the Middle Ages* (Oxford: Clarendon Press, 1936 [first publ. 1895]), vol. I, ch. 2.

to be beyond human comprehension, and, in the end, of committing theological heresy. A church council condemned his views, and he was eventually forbidden to teach. But the traditional trivium teachers were losing students to the dialecticians, and the nurturing friendships between students and spiritual mentors were giving way to an atmosphere of free inquiry and strident contention. Abelard was in effect a progenitor of the University of Paris.[2]

His influence remained, and within ten years Peter Lombard of the Notre Dame cathedral school published a collection of sometimes conflicting opinions from church fathers and medieval theologians similar to *Sic et Non*. But Lombard's work, the *Sentences,* avoided both the dialectical contentiousness of Abelard and the authoritarian dogmatism of some of his opponents. It became the standard theology textbook until the sixteenth century, as well as the starting point for doctrinal disputations and the subject of numerous commentaries. The development of dialectical skills was becoming a major pedagogical objective, even in theological education.

The major catalyst for change in the thirteenth-century university was related to this development. Up until this point, Christian scholars knew little of Aristotle's work beyond his writings about dialectic; his works on deductive logic, the sciences, metaphysics, and ethics were only known in the Moslem world. In the twelfth and thirteenth centuries, however, Latin translations from Greek and Arabic appeared, only to be greeted with grave suspicion because they seemed to contradict Christian theology. Bonaventure, for instance, preached sermons on the dangers to the faith found in Aristotle's philosophy, arguing that without divine illumination pagans could not be sure of the

2. See John Marenbon, *The Philosophy of Peter Abelard* (Cambridge: Cambridge Univ. Press, 1997).

truth, and at the University of Paris the teaching of Aristotle's metaphysics and natural philosophy was for a while officially banned.

Not everyone agreed with the condemnation of Aristotle, however. Thomas Aquinas carefully studied Aristotle for himself and found much that was not only compatible with Christian thought but helpful to it as well. He wrote commentaries on a number of Aristotle's major works, and incorporated many of the philosopher's key ideas into his own teaching and thinking. Dialectic (later to be known as the "old logic") had been a helpful tool for analyzing and interpreting texts, but Aristotle's "new logic" of the syllogism made it possible to demonstrate the truth or falsity of propositions. Knowing the truth was even more important to Aquinas than simply understanding a text — especially now that Moslem thought was intruding into the West — and it was far more to the point than the cynical rhetoric with which disillusioned scholars attacked ignorant clerics and pedantic dialecticians.

Education, according to Aquinas, should develop the God-given capacity to know what is true and good. Truth is the aim of what he called "speculative science," and good is the aim of "moral science." In children, of course, care for the body, and the cultivation of moral virtues that will help them discipline their physical appetites, come first. Nevertheless, to discipline and develop mental capacities, logic is basic, and in it he includes all the trivium, following not the literary approach of Augustine and the monastery schools but a dialectical emphasis more like Abelard's. The remaining liberal arts (the quadrivium) should follow: they afford a basis for grasping the universal forms of natural entities (natural philosophy) and the underlying forms of mathematics that Augustine had uncovered. This in turn leads to the one source of all created order and truth, the divine Logos, and so to metaphysics and theology. Moral science, meanwhile, will foster personal virtues and explain why they are essential to the common good.[3]

Aquinas also argued that the mechanical arts, including medicine, law, and agriculture, are like moral science in that they too involve an active life for the common good. And what about teaching? Is it a contemplative or an active life, Thomas asks? Does it deal in eternal verities or in temporal affairs? With the decline of monastery schools and the church's uncertain confidence in a university, this was an important question, and Aquinas's response is measured. Teaching, he says, has a twofold subject matter, and the verb "to teach" has two accusatives. If we consider the art or science that is taught, then it is a contemplative life devoted to the truth; but if we consider students and their needs, then it is indeed an active life engaged in the affairs of this world for the common good.[4] It is not a choice between the two, for with a duty to both the discipline and the student, the teacher should in reality be always a teacher-scholar.

In teaching students as in working with apprentices, then, a teacher must teach his pupils how to discover and know the truth. He does this by showing how he himself approaches the science and then giving them practice in doing it themselves. In teaching textual analysis, for example, he demonstrates how he organizes in rational terms all the particulars observed in a text and then has them try it, for as rational beings they too have the capacity to seek truth. According to Aquinas we need not assume any innate knowledge, as Plato did, nor presume that truth is accessible independent of any preconditions. A God-given mind,

---

3. *The Division and Methods of the Sciences,* translated by Armand Maurer from Thomas' commentary on Boethius' *De Trinitate* (Leiden: E. J. Brill, 1986). Compare Pierre H. Conway and Benedict M. Ashley, *The Liberal Arts in St. Thomas Aquinas* (Washington, D.C.: Thomist Press, 1959).

4. Thomas Aquinas, *Truth,* trans. J. McGlynn (Chicago: Henry Regnery Co., 1953), q.11, art. iv.

however, has the potential to become an active intellect in possession of the truth, and teaching assists the actualization of that potential. No special divine illumination such as Bonaventure invoked is needed, for the God-given light of active reason is sufficient for understanding the natural order and then drawing both metaphysical and ethical implications.

Developing this capacity for logical thinking required going beyond the literary studies and allegorical interpretation that had dominated earlier learning to a teaching by means of logically organized disputations. The format of Aquinas's *Summa Theologica* illustrates this. A huge compendium, it is organized as a series of "questions" for debate, each subdivided into several parts or "articles." Each article starts with "objections" to what the question seems to suggest, followed by a statement "on the contrary," then an extended "I answer that . . . ," and finally an "I reply" to each of the objections. Simple affirmations or denials are avoided; reasons are always given, sometimes using a reference to an authoritative text, and sometimes a logical inference from premises generally agreed upon or previously demonstrated. Aquinas's method shows how the teacher argues for the truth of his convictions, and provides the reader with endless practice in rationally organized thinking and deductive logic — in addition to putting the liberal arts and philosophy to work in theological studies. This was the kind of education that characterized thirteenth-century scholasticism, in contrast to the pattern set by monastery and cathedral schools.

Aquinas was convinced that the inner teleology that makes learning possible extends throughout the creation. Everything has its God-given nature; an object has not only material elements and causal forces, nor only the unchanging form of a species, but also a "final" cause, the inner potential for whatever natural end God intended it within his creation. This in effect is what Aristotle had said in his *Physics* and elsewhere, but Aquinas adds what he learned from Augustine, that creation reveals the archetypal wisdom and goodness of God. Instead of Augustine's rhetorical and literary approach, however, Aquinas emphasizes logic and the sciences. Natural science provides the premises for his arguments for God's existence, it builds up faith and devotion by contemplating the wisdom, power, and goodness of the creator, and it provides an apologetic by helping to refute errors.[5]

Thomas was also concerned about the moral development of students and shared the medieval distrust of mere curiosity, fearing that it could become self-indulgent, feed intellectual pride, or draw one away from the truth. He distinguished a proper studiousness from one that loves the pursuit of knowledge more than it loves truth. The pursuit of knowledge can be either right or wrong: seeking knowledge in order to sin is plainly wrong, but so too is pursuing a less important study to the neglect of a more important one or ignoring God as the source and end of knowledge and truth. Knowledge brings with it moral responsibility for the wise and good use of both abilities and knowledge.[6] Not only moral virtues but also intellectual virtues like wisdom and prudence are essential in Christian learning.[7]

The culmination of university education, Aquinas believed, is theology. Natural philosophy is the prelude to a science of first principles underlying both the natural and the moral sciences, namely metaphysics, which evidences the wisdom and goodness of God. Theology is accordingly the queen of the sciences, with philosophy and liberal learning as her handmaidens.[8] It teaches the practical wisdom of judging human affairs by God's laws and directing human life by his purposes, and

---

5. Thomas Aquinas, *Summa Contra Gentiles*, Bk. II, ch. 2-4.
6. Thomas Aquinas, *Summa Theologica*, II-II, q.167.
7. See Aquinas, *S.T.*, I-II, q.57.
8. Aquinas, *S.T.*, I, q.1.

contemplates reason's highest good, the wisdom and goodness of God himself.

But if theology is a science, what happens to the symbolic and mystical tradition that Abelard had criticized? Should "holy teaching," as Aquinas calls it, use metaphorical or symbolic language that appeals to the senses, or should it appeal instead to reason? Scripture uses metaphor and allegory, he observes,[9] because all knowledge must begin with sense experience, and because the uneducated are not ready for abstract intellectual truths without sensory ingredients. Since a literal sense underlies the metaphors and allegories, God is still known, however imperfectly. Moreover, theology is different from other sciences, because they deal with general kinds of things so that we gradually learn to think in theoretical terms about the universals in different species, yet God is not a member of any species. There is but one God, and he is unique. So theology speaks of him either negatively (by what he is not) or by analogies based on the essential properties of all being: he is the perfect being, goodness and truth itself which created things image to whatever degree they are able. They all participate in that hierarchy of beauty and goodness, which, like a cosmic choreographed dance, displays the glories of its creator.

What then is reason's role in relation to revelation? The distinction is sharper now that reason is more logical and scientific, and the means of revelation not as dominantly symbolic. Moreover, God illuminates the mind by the light of reason, so it may well know some truths about him without any special revelation. It can, for instance, discover first principles of the faith, such as God's existence, and something of his unity and goodness or other essential attributes. Aquinas was well aware that reason is limited and that some mysteries of the faith are known only by

9. Aquinas, *S.T.*, I, q.1, art. 9-10.

divine revelation. While God reveals much that reason by itself cannot discover, however, reason may still understand such truths of faith, however imperfectly, and can often construct supportive arguments of a "probable" sort. In no way are revelation and reason either opposed or mutually exclusive. On the contrary, Thomas reminds us, reason is by its nature adapted to knowing truth, including truths of faith. The light of reason and the light of revelation are both God's gifts, both are concerned with truth, and truth is ultimately one. All truth is God's truth, no matter where or by what means it is found.

These matters came into focus when the unity of truth was challenged at the University of Paris. Some of the younger masters of arts started teaching that a belief can be true in philosophy the contradictory of which is true in theology. The issue arose because a Moslem philosopher named Averroes took Aristotle to deny individual immortality on the grounds that all humans share one universal soul in common to them all. The Christian Averroists agreed with this interpretation and compounded the problem by further agreeing with Aristotle that the world was made from eternal materials rather than created in time out of nothing. Creation in time, they argued, would imply that God changed his mind, and that would be totally unfitting for one all-wise.

The controversy this provoked challenged any and every Christian use of Aristotle's science and philosophy. Bonaventure in particular did not want him taught in the university, since the divine illumination that is necessary in such matters comes only to the faithful. Aquinas, on the other hand, was more cautious, for how could truths revealed by God conflict with truths gained by God-given reason? Aristotle's first principle of logic, the law of non-contradiction, in fact affirmed that a belief and its contradictory simply cannot both be true at the same time — so somewhere the Averroist argument must have gone wrong.

The scholastic method proved its worth. Aquinas had recently studied Aristotle's work *On the Soul,* and now he subjected it to a close textual analysis that contradicted the Averroist interpretation. Since Aristotle clearly said no soul could exist except in a particular body, how could there be but one universal soul in common for all persons? And God could not have changed his mind when he created the world in time, because the Augustinian teaching about eternal exemplars in the mind of God means that he would have known about it eternally. So, Aquinas argued, Aristotle requires neither an eternal creation nor the denial of individual souls as some had thought.[10]

The outcome of all this debate was mixed, however, for people do not quickly change their minds about what they fear. Thomas's use of Aristotelian science did arouse philosophical opposition to Averroism, and contributed to its official condemnation in 1270. As Aquinas said, the study of creation is both theologically instructive and useful apologetically in confronting error. Nevertheless, guilt by association continued to plague Christian Aristotelians and seriously curbed their freedom in teaching for the next half century. Moreover, their scientific and logical emphasis remained at variance with the humanist tradition that the Renaissance would revive, until the scientific revolution brought conflicts of science and religion to the fore once again.

10. See Ralph McInerny, *Aquinas Against the Averroists* (West Lafayette, Ind.: Purdue Univ. Press, 1993).

SIX

The Reformation
and the Usefulness
of Liberal Arts

About two hundred years after its emergence, the scholastic approach to education was challenged by the Renaissance revival of classical learning. Impressed by Cicero's ideal of *studia humanitatis,* scholars began turning to classical languages and literature, emphasizing poetry and rhetoric rather than formal logic, and ethics and politics rather than metaphysics. Wishing to refine the mind and care for the soul, they valued the power of rhetoric in extolling virtue and of poetry in charming the emotions. Eloquent wisdom — rather than the logical training with which scholasticism prepared students for theology or the law — was again the focus of education.

The teaching method of the scholastics had become basically the disputation with its syllogistic reasoning. This *via nova,* as it was called, was now challenged by the *via antiqua* of literary exposition. As early as 1456, Peter Luder used his inaugural address at Heidelberg to spell out an educational program based on the classical literature of antiquity, particularly rhetoric, poetry, and history.[1] Elsewhere Ockholm's nominalism sparked debate about the study of logic as preparation for metaphysics and theology; his denial of real universals contradicted the metaphysics on which scholastic theology had depended and emphasized the gap between reason and revelation. But humanists were more interested in the dialectic used by rhetoricians than in syllogisms. Peter Ramus argued that Aristotle's logic was unnatural and artificial, and he developed a "natural," informal logic of the human mind to take its place. Scholastics at the University of Paris were so irate when Ramus's work first appeared that they suppressed his books and forbade him to teach. Later he became a Protestant and was killed in the St. Bartholomew's Eve massacre of 1572, but by then his informal logic was finding wide acceptance among humanist educators. Focusing on the content of literature rather than rhetorical style alone, it emphasized practical uses of language and argument that appealed also to the new merchant class.

The main contribution of humanist learning, however, was its usefulness in the study of Scripture, in contrast to an abstruse scholastic theology grounded in metaphysics. They brought to their study of the Bible a rich knowledge of ancient languages and literature, and in the light of that learning they began to rethink the traditional theology of their times. They also undertook to reform education because they wanted the laity to read and understand Scripture for themselves and to be prepared for their callings in society. Luther put it plainly: "Where are the preachers, jurists and physicians to come from, if grammar and other rhetorical arts are not taught?"[2]

1. James H. Overfield, *Humanism and Scholasticism in Late Medieval Germany* (Princeton, N.J.: Princeton Univ. Press, 1984), pp. 65-68.

2. "A Sermon on Keeping Children in School," in *Luther's Works: The Christian in Society*, ed. Robert C. Schultz (Philadelphia: Fortress Press, 1963), vol. 46, p. 252.

Erasmus set the pace both as a humanist and as an educational reformer. His early schooling and the time he spent in an Augustinian monastery convinced him that he needed to study original texts rather than accept the secondhand or thirdhand ideas in scholastic commentaries. He made the acquaintance of humanists while studying theology in Paris, and as a tutor he wrote manuals on the liberal arts for his students. At Cambridge he met the humanist and theologian, John Colet, who interested him in biblical scholarship and enlisted his assistance against scholastic theologians at Oxford who resisted the biblically based approach. When Huguenots and Jesuits had to flee persecution in France, he helped establish a new college at Louvain for the study of sacred languages. He himself was more the classical scholar than a theologian or activist reformer, however; he translated Greek and Latin authors, edited the works of St. Jerome, the church father, and produced a critical edition of the Greek New Testament text along with a Latin translation that became the basis for Luther's German translation. He also repeatedly advocated a humanist education for all social classes, both men and women, for their intellectual and moral development. This, not scholasticism, was what he believed an urban and literate society needed.

The manuals he wrote for students recommended authors they should study and methods they should follow, such as compiling a "common place book" of useful quotations on various topics. His own compilation, *Adagia,* recorded over eight hundred wise adages from classical writers. His *Copia* was for a long time the standard rhetoric text in universities throughout northern Europe, while his *Antibarbari,* an early version of which he had shown to John Colet, was written in a classic satirical style and defended classical learning. The barbarians, he reports, complain that classical authors are heathen and licentious and, in addition, are difficult to understand — complaints Christian educators since the early church have repeatedly faced. Erasmus suggests these opponents of classical learning may not even have read the material for themselves, and he argues that if we inherit other useful things from pagans, then why not their arts as well? Whatever wisdom pagans discover depends on God, who is Wisdom itself.

> Every thing in the pagan world that was valiantly done, brilliantly said, ingeniously thought, diligently transmitted, has been prepared by Christ for his society. He it is who supplied the intellect, who added the zest for inquiry, and it was through him alone that they found what they sought. Their age produced the harvest of creative work, not so much for them as for us. . . . But the highest good, the perfect gift, was reserved by Christ for his own time.[3]

It may be true that none of these liberal arts are Christian, for they neither deal with Christ nor were invented by Christians, but nonetheless they all concern him. Erasmus cites references to "spoiling the Egyptians" from both Jerome and Augustine's *On Christian Doctrine* and then claims that Paul's liberal learning prepared him for debate in Athens. And where else did John get that sublime statement about the Logos in John 1:1?

The *Antibarbari* was only Erasmus's first manifesto. In the introduction to his Latin translation of the New Testament, he declares that the philosophy of Christ is revealed both in the written Word and the Word incarnate and is not just for monks and theologians. The Christian vocation is for all. Nor is the love of

---

3. *Collected Works of Erasmus,* ed. Craig R. Thompson (Toronto: Univ. of Toronto Press, 1978), vol. 46, p. 60. Compare Bruce A. Kimball, *Orators and Philosophers: A History of the Idea of Liberal Education* (New York: Teachers College Press, 1986), pp. 87-89.

learning for pleasure only, but for the sake of Christ. For these two reasons, the Bible must be available in the common language of the people, available for the kind of reflective, expository study humanist schools teach.

This is where Erasmus's and Martin Luther's concerns met: they agreed on the value of humanistic education for laity if they were to read the Bible in their own language. As a classical scholar, however, Erasmus respected the antiquity of an interpretation (he constantly quoted the church father Jerome) and particularly respected a consensus of the faithful. As a theologian, Luther looked to Augustine rather than Jerome, although he opposed allegorical interpretations however ancient (calling them "theological juggling"). He instead brought an overall theological understanding of the Scriptures to his study of a text. So while Erasmus depended on linguistic tools alone, and submitted to church authority in other matters, Luther relied on an inner certainty of faith based on the Bible alone, whatever the church might say.

Luther had studied Aristotle's logic and science at the university in Erfurt, which like the older German universities was dominated by nominalism. This probably accounts for the fact that at one stage seventeen of the twenty-two books required at Erfurt for the B.A. examination were on logic while none were on rhetoric. The scholastic dominance did not remain unchallenged by humanism, however, and the German princes began to support the revival of classical "letters," so that between 1515 and 1535 the scholastics gradually lost their hold on the universities. Over a period of seven years the enrollment at Erfurt dropped from 311 to only 13 students. In those places where schools under scholastic control failed to change, the nobility took the initiative and founded colleges of humanistic studies that taught the logic of Ramus. With curricular change, ancient languages and literature were introduced and teaching by means of logical disputations ceased.[4] Peter Luder may have posed the idea, but Wittenberg provided the needful spark.

After completing the master's degree in 1505, Luther joined an Augustinian monastic order and studied the nominalist theology of Gabriel Biel before moving to Wittenberg in 1508 to teach. At first he lectured on Aristotle's logic, physics, and ethics, later on Scripture and on Lombard's *Sentences,* which was still the standard theology textbook. His nominalism had ruled out the metaphysical groundwork for scholastic theology, but now his spiritual struggles increasingly underscored the gulf between that approach to theology and the gospel, so that even nominalist logic seemed sterile. He found the older dialectic preferable, for it "speaks simply, straightforwardly and plainly."[5] In 1517 he wrote ninety-seven theses for a student to defend, a "Disputation against Scholastic Theology," opposing the claim that Aristotle and his logic were essential for studying theology. Trinitarian doctrine is not subject to syllogistic proof, he argued, but is an object of faith.

Luther's fullest statement about higher education is his 1520 "Letter to the Christian Nobility and the German Nation concerning the Reform of the Christian Estate." The universities, he declares, need a thorough reformation because the blind, heathen Aristotle rules them far more than Christ. So he advises discarding not only the *Physics* and *Metaphysics,* but also the *Nichomachean Ethics,* because it opposes divine grace and Christian virtues. While the *Logic, Rhetoric,* and *Poetics* should be retained in abridged form, for their usefulness in training young people to speak and preach properly, the most useful studies for

4. See Overfield, *Humanism and Scholasticism,* ch. 8.

5. *The Table-Talk of Martin Luther,* trans. and ed. William Hazlitt (London: George Bell and Sons, 1884), p. 339. See also B. A. Gerish, *Grace and Reason: A Study in the Theology of Luther* (Oxford: Clarendon Press, 1962); Gerhard Ebeling, *Luther, An Introduction to His Thought* (Philadelphia: Fortress Press, 1970).

propagating Christianity are history, grammar, and ancient languages. History is "the teacher of life" that stirs emotions more than cold logic and, while dialectic helps one speak plainly and guides the understanding to truth, rhetoric adorns speech and persuades the will. But the Bible should be the most important reading material for every person, and libraries should always include Scriptures in both original and modern languages. No work, he concludes, is more worthy of pope or emperor than a thorough reform of universities, for it is there that the young people with whom the future of Christianity lies are educated.

Like Augustine, Luther valued humanist learning primarily for its usefulness in biblical studies and the work of the church, but the German princes also foresaw its usefulness in commerce and other princely affairs. Wittenberg's patron, the elector Frederick, solicited advice from several professors, including the dean of the theology faculty, Luther himself, and in 1518 a new curriculum was introduced that included both Greek and Hebrew. As professor of Greek, Luther hired the young Philip Melanchthon, whose inaugural address on "The Improvement of Studies" deplored scholasticism's focus on commentaries and called for the study of original languages and literature. Other German universities followed the precedent, and by mid-century humanist learning dominated German higher education. Luther and Melanchthon also developed proposals for elementary education in the liberal arts that were later enacted into law, producing the first Protestant school system.

Although Luther emphasized the usefulness of liberal learning in both church and society, he was not optimistic about any further relationship between faith and learning. Human reason, he allowed, can show that God exists and that he is able to help us, but it cannot reveal who he is or that he is willing to help. Its main functions are in temporal affairs rather than in contemplating eternal truths in the mind of God or tracing the unity of truth

— a crucial change from both monastery schools and scholastic universities. Luther's nominalist background was involved here since, if universal terms only designate similar particulars rather than eternal realities, then human reason is basically equipped only for earthly affairs. Unresolved tensions will remain, and Luther's two kingdom theology found expression in the relationship between faith and secular learning generally as well as in the relationship between logic and theology. He refused to integrate them in an overall logical system as the scholastics did.

This is where his view of learning differs most from John Calvin's. Educated in the arts faculty at the University of Paris, Calvin too studied Aristotelian logic and science and the theology of Peter Lombard, but he developed a love for classical and humanist learning while studying law at Orleans and Bruges. He wrote a commentary on Seneca's *De Clementia,* tracing similarities between Stoic and Christian ethics, and his *Institutes of the Christian Religion,* written at the age of twenty-six, cites freely from philosophers and poets, pagan as well as Christian, while his biblical commentaries show a blend of scholastic and humanist influences.

In 1541, concerned about the ignorance and superstition he observed after coming to Geneva to assist the struggling reforms already underway there, Calvin issued a statement on church polity which included the need for a college to prepare young people for the ministry and for civil government.[6] At the opening ceremony of the Geneva academy nearly eighteen years later, Theodore Beza, Calvin's former Greek teacher who became rector of the Geneva Academy, told the students that they were "to become inbred of true religion and equipped with all good arts,

6. See Gillian Lewis, "The Geneva Academy," in *Calvinism in Europe, 1540 to 1620,* ed. Andrew Pettegree et al. (Cambridge: Cambridge Univ. Press, 1994), ch. 3. See also essays by W. Stanford Reid and T. M. Moore in Richard Gamble (ed.), *Articles on Calvin and Calvinism,* vol. 3 (New York: Garland Publ. Co., 1992).

the better to amplify God's glory." The academy included a preparatory school and mechanical arts as well as providing a humanist university education. A thorough knowledge of classical languages was required of all, as was advanced work in rhetoric that used both Aristotle and Cicero, and theology was taught both by the exposition of biblical literature and by scholastic disputation. Since Calvin regarded the liberal arts as God-given to make "terrestrial" activities possible, the Geneva academy developed faculties of theology, law, and medicine, for all of which the liberal arts were prerequisite.

Calvin's overall aim was "wise and eloquent piety," not the distorted wisdom of the world but the wisdom of our creator. The wisdom of the world, he notes in his commentary on First Corinthians, does not refer to the liberal arts, for they depend on truth that is the same for all people in all times and places, as Augustine showed. They may have come down to us from the heathen, but we are at liberty to borrow from any source anything that came from God. All truth has its source in him. Rationalistic dogmatism was another matter. A sixteenth-century Hutterite tract had asked "Why are there no university graduates in our midst?," asserting that intellectual sophistication kills the simplicity of faith, and the Hutterites took Paul's comments about "destroying arguments" (2 Cor. 10:5) to mean that logic has no place in spiritual understanding.[7] Calvin, on the other hand, took "philosophy and vain deceit" (Col. 2:8) to refer to intellectual pride, a kind of idolatry or self-worship that sometimes characterized both intramural disputes between scholastics and their current criticism that humanists were uneducated; he did not see it as referring to logic or learning as such.

7. "Reason and Obedience," in *The Mennonite Encyclopedia: A Comprehensive Reference Work on the Anabaptist-Mennonite Movement,* vol. IV (Hillsboro, Kans.: Mennonite Brethren Publ. House, 1959).

> There cannot be found the least particle of wisdom, light, righteousness, power, rectitude, or sincere truth that does not proceed from him [God], and claim him as its author.[8]

Calvin's *Institutes of the Christian Religion* develops the theological basis for his views on education. A first version had appeared before he came to Geneva, but the definitive edition became available in 1541. In contrast to the scholastics, who proceeded from the liberal arts to metaphysics and thence to theology, Calvin starts by observing that the seed of religion is inscribed on every heart. Even the illiterate have a sense of the deity, for they see the order in creation and admire God's workmanship. Those adept in the liberal arts, however, can investigate the divine wisdom; precision and skill in astronomy, for instance, clearly reveal his providence and lift the mind to contemplate his glory.

> The manifold ability of the soul enables it to take a survey of heaven and earth; to join the past to the present; to retain the memory of things heard long ago; to conceive whatever it chooses by the help of imagination; its ingenuity also in the invention of such admirable arts, — are certain proofs of the divinity in man.[9]

God created us in his own image and after his likeness, with a right understanding, "affections regulated by reason," and the senses properly ordered. He made us rational beings, capable of discerning good and evil and endowed with free will. The seeds of liberal learning and social order are therefore innate in hu-

8. John Calvin, *Institutes of the Christian Religion,* trans. John Wilson (Grand Rapids: Eerdmans, 1949), I.ii.2.
9. Calvin, *Institutes,* I.v.5.

mankind without any instructor or legislator.[10] The term "seeds" suggests that the capacity to learn is akin to the "seed" of religion, for both are implicit in the image of God. It echoes Seneca's Stoic notion of *logoi spermatikoi* by which God shaped natural law, and Calvin took the Decalogue to reiterate natural moral laws implicit in the creation. Moreover, if Adam named the animals he must have discovered their distinctive natures, and so from the beginning God intended scientific inquiry and other cultural activities. These too are rooted in the natural order. The liberal arts and sciences, along with domestic economy and civil society, are all included in the creation mandate.

Now, however, reason is partly debilitated, the will is fettered by unruly desires, and we grope our way through various errors. Even so, there remains some desire to learn, some clarity of mind, some love of truth, so that in the liberal arts and sciences or in the mechanical arts or in political and economic affairs order can often prevail. In "celestial" things like a true knowledge of God and his grace, however, the wisest of men are "blinder than moles." In matters of ethics, sinful desire too easily ignores the natural order and follows its own inclinations. Only restoration to the image of Christ, the perfect man, will suffice.[11]

With much of this Luther would agree, but Calvin's distinction between the terrestrial and the celestial, and thereby between faith and learning, goes beyond Luther's two kingdoms. Calvin sees them both as being still under the sovereignty of Christ, the lord of all creation. Moreover, the role of reason was more constructive in the Stoic tradition of Cicero and Seneca that Calvin admired than in the nominalism that influenced Luther. Calvin's mission for Christian learning seems more positive than Luther's because he roots it in the creation mandate as af-

10. Calvin, *Institutes,* II.ii.13. See also I.xv.
11. Calvin, *Institutes,* II.xii-xviii.

fected by sin and grace. They both address the care of the soul and the usefulness of the liberal arts, but Calvin has a stronger emphasis on the unity of truth and thereby on the doxological result. In his commentary on John's Gospel, he translates *logos* by the Latin *sermo* (a discourse) rather than *verbum* (a word), because he understands Jesus to be God's eternal wisdom for the whole of creation rather than just one particular utterance. He agrees with Augustine that God created in the light of a wise conception of the entire order of things summed up in the eternal Logos. He also assumes that the light of the Logos (John 1:9) is reason, but, because reason's light is darkened by sin, the redemption afforded by the incarnate Logos must also illumine learning. The Christian scholar can, in the words of the Westminster Confession, "glorify God and enjoy him" in scholarship because creation, sin, and grace affect human learning as they do everything else.

Humanism, and particularly Calvin's Christian humanism, profoundly affected English universities. As early as the thirteenth century, Robert Grosseteste had introduced mathematics and science at Oxford University with a Platonic rather than an Aristotelian emphasis, and rather than submitting differences in biblical interpretation to scholastic disputations he appealed to the original languages. In the 1530s Henry VIII called for fewer scholastic textbooks, replacing them with ancient languages, rhetoric, and humanist learning. His dissolution of the monasteries dissolved both the monastery schools and monastic houses at the universities. Scholasticism lost strength, and in 1550 the writings of Duns Scotus were burned in public at Oxford. Well before that some of Erasmus's ideals were being recognized at Cambridge, where divinity lectures were required to focus on the true sense of Scripture and were forbidden to follow the manner of scholastic controversies; at Cambridge also Melanchthon was a prescribed author because of his attention to Greek as well as

Latin. In addition, the humanists disliked the technicalities of canon law, and their emphasis on the moral purpose of education gave a greater role to laymen in both church and society. Aristotelian logic was replaced by Ramus's more informal reasoning, and new humanist colleges sprang up to better educate clergy and laity alike. The practical benefits of these changes appealed to the lay gentry, England's ruling class, and to the growing merchant class that included many Puritans. Influenced by Calvin's theology and his example at Geneva, they too stressed the cultivation of wise and eloquent piety.[12]

In Scotland John Knox also drew a close connection between reformation and education, and his 1560 *Book of Discipline* proposed a national education plan to provide church and state with qualified leaders. In the main towns, colleges were to teach classical languages and the liberal arts, preparing all people for a trade and the more capable for university. The universities of Glasgow, Aberdeen, and St. Andrews all began to reform, and new colleges were founded on the model of Calvin's Geneva academy.[13] Humanist education would prevail, especially in Protestant countries, at least until the Enlightenment.

12. H. C. Porter, *Reformation and Reaction in Tudor Cambridge* (Hamden, Conn.: Archon Books, 1972); Hugh Kearney, *Scholars and Gentlemen: Universities and Society in Pre-Industrial Britain, 1500-1700* (Ithaca, N.Y.: Cornell Univ. Press, 1970).

13. Douglas Sloan, *The Scottish Enlightenment and the American College Ideal* (New York: Teachers College Press, 1971).

SEVEN

Francis Bacon: Modern Science and the Uses of Knowledge

The Protestant Reformation and classical humanism continued to affect higher education in the seventeenth century, but the scientific revolution, by then begun, would have educational consequences that reach to the present day. During the Elizabethan age in England, both scholastic and classical humanist educators had been criticized for ignoring the new science, but the dissatisfaction found its most effective voice in Francis Bacon, the Lord Chancellor of England under the first Stuart king, James I. A statesmanlike Renaissance man, he published in 1605 *The Advancement of Learning,* a critique of the educational status quo, and in 1620 his *Novum Organum* proposed a new empirical methodology to replace Aristotle's *Organon,* which contained his logic. Envisioning new uses for the new scientific knowledge, he exercised an increasing influence throughout the seventeenth century and into the Enlightenment and Industrial Revolution that followed. The Reformers wanted classical learning to serve the church, while Bacon wanted future learning to serve society.

Bacon had studied Aristotle and Greek science as an undergraduate at Cambridge, and like others he found much of it uninspiring and sterile. The logic might be useful in civil matters that depend on arguing one's opinions, but it was not subtle enough to deal with the stubborn facts of nature: disputations are idle exercises when they demonstrate by logic what we already know from experience. Scholastic metaphysics enunciated general principles by abstracting them from particulars, but the particulars themselves received no attention or else attempts to deal with them became hopelessly embroiled in disputes. As a result, the Aristotelian sciences stood like statues, worshipped and celebrated but never advancing; scholars settled their questions by exchanging one doctrine for another, but in reality they never changed a thing. Natural theology was a perfect example: believers had no need for it, yet they argued in abstraction over its persuasiveness while unbelievers remained unconvinced. Meanwhile, two thousand years of Aristotelianism had failed to restore humankind's dominion over the creation, and Bacon was disgusted at so much wasted effort.

Classical humanism had increasingly displaced scholasticism in education. The study of classical languages and literature had opened up the Scriptures, and renewed attention to rhetoric had transformed preaching. But Bacon was less than enthusiastic: the humanists' books endlessly repeated the same thing in different ways and, while studying history might make one wise, poetry make one witty, and mathematics make one subtle, that was scant benefit from liberal learning in Bacon's opinion. He saw humanists as more interested in words than facts, as obsessed with verbal ornamentation and display; the wisdom they purported to teach issued only in words, not works. In all the succession of masters and teachers, none were inventors — except in the mechanical arts. Empirical observation never reached beyond a simple enumeration of instances, and so was barely distinguishable from the popular superstitions that preyed on the populace.[1] Consequently, neither humanism nor scholasticism was providing the new knowledge which that age of discovery desired and which the scientific revolution could provide.

Bacon pointed an accusing finger at three "vanities": the "contentious learning" of scholastic disputations which demonstrate only one's logical power over opponents; the "delicate learning" of humanists who toy pointlessly with beautiful words rather than with matters of substance; and the "fantastical learning" of alchemists and astrologers who seek to influence nature without knowing how it really functions. These three wasted exercises are either devoid of truth, hence false, or devoid of usefulness, hence frivolous. They appeal to either credulity or curiosity — and idle curiosity had long been regarded as a vice rather than an intellectual virtue. Bacon proposed to change all three.[2]

His mother was a devout Calvinist, and Bacon himself used prayers that reflected Reformed influences. A Reformed influence is also evident in what he saw as the ultimate goal of human knowledge, "the glory of the Creator and the relief of man's estate." He refers repeatedly to the creation mandate, insisting that God gifted us with reason to facilitate our authority over nature, but that out of ambition and pride we chose instead to use it (or neglect it) for other ends.

> For man by the fall fell at the same time from his state of innocency and from his dominion over creation. Both of these losses however can even in this life be in some part repaired; the former by religion and faith, the latter by arts and sciences.[3]

1. See Bacon's *Advancement of Learning* and the Preface to his *Novum Organum* in *Essays, Advancement of Learning, New Atlantis, and Other Pieces,* ed. R. F. Jones (New York: Odyssey Press, 1937).
2. Bacon, *Advancement of Learning*, p. 198.
3. Bacon, *Novum Organum*, Aphorism II.52.

Both faith and learning could help improve the human condition.

In *The Advancement of Learning,* Bacon points out the necessity of finding a more effective conjunction of contemplation and action. Creation manifests both the attributes and the actions of God, the wisdom of its order and the power that made it be. This is the archetype to follow:[4] contemplate the wisdom in nature's ordering, and for acting use the power that knowledge provides. The medievals could be content to contemplate, but for a Reformed believer like Bacon contemplation brought a call to work. His view of work as a creation mandate undergirded his vision of science "for the glory of the Creator and the relief of man's estate."

But if education was to be organized to that end, some initial changes (remarkably familiar) would be needed. Teachers, for example, had become so professionalized in theology, law, or medicine that none attended to the arts and sciences as such but only to their own particular professions, and this handicapped the advancement of science. Salaries were insufficient to attract able scholars, and no resources were available for conducting experiments. Logic and rhetoric were taught too soon in the curriculum, before students had sufficient maturity and experience to use them effectively. More discussion of the educational process was therefore necessary, as well as broader consultations with European universities.[5] This was a statesmanlike vision.

More significant by far were Bacon's inductive methods for exploring order in the creation, because if we can trace the causal regularities of fixed natural laws then we can use them to control natural processes for human benefit. He likened Aristotle's method of working deductively from universal first principles to

---

4. Bacon, *Advancement,* p. 214.
5. Bacon, *Advancement,* book 2.

the spider making cobwebs out of its own substance, and compared the naive observations of some new scientists to miscellaneous scraps of food collected by an ant. He considered his inductive method, on the other hand, to be like the busy bee which gathers material from flowers but then digests and transforms it into something new and useful.[6] Carefully used inductive methods will yield predictable results, the same for everybody, a universal kind of knowledge, he claimed, and his *New Atlantis* envisioned the scientific utopia which might result.

Notice how radical is the educational change he proposes. Higher education would no longer be just the transmission of knowledge and values inherited from the past, but also research and the discovery of new knowledge. He denies any intention of preventing existing arts and sciences from "encouraging discussion, adorning discourses or being employed serviceably in common life,"[7] but he introduces a much stronger utilitarian view of learning with emphasis on material benefits rather than on the intellectual, moral, and spiritual formation of students.

Notice too that the content of science changes with the method. "Archetypes" are no longer eternal exemplars in the mind of God, but simply the divine wisdom and power directly displayed in creation. "Forms" are no longer abstract universals, but fixed causal laws. Bacon was a nominalist who rejected the theory of forms and the teleological worldview that accompanied it: final causes corrupt the sciences, except those having to do with human actions.[8] He therefore assigns consideration of final causes to theology and frees science to consider nature's mechanisms, its material and efficient causes alone.

Notice particularly his desire for a knowledge everybody can

6. Bacon, *Novum Organum*, Aphorism I.95 and, for his methods, bk. II.
7. Bacon, *Novum Organum*, Aphorism I.128.
8. Bacon, *Novum Organum*, Aphorisms II.1-3.

agree on. It would become the Enlightenment ideal of knowledge that is universally the same, independent of preconceptions and religious differences. Bacon believed that we are directly aware of physical things (Descartes's theory of indirect or representative perception had not yet taken over), and so subjective ideas could be excluded and knowledge could be wholly objective. To further ensure it, he renounced four possible subjective influences: individual prejudices (which he calls idols of the cave), verbal associations (idols of the market place), cultural assumptions (idols of the tribe), and philosophical preconceptions (idols of the theater). Turning from such idols, objective science can exercise its God-given authority over nature and transform the human condition.[9]

We can readily see why this had such appeal. The Renaissance had resurrected an array of ancient philosophies: Platonism, Stoicism, and Democritan materialism, each with its own traditional account of nature. The Reformation had created a vacuum of authority in matters on which Scripture is silent, and Protestantism was torn by differing interpretations of the Bible. The political order was questioned, too. Everywhere the need seemed obvious for an objective, universally assured knowledge independent of divisive beliefs. Bacon's secretary, Thomas Hobbes, would later use the Baconian method to provide an objective scientific basis for political authority, and even biblical interpretation came to be treated like Baconian science. The Enlightenment's "light of reason" was really the light of science, and its "rule of reason" the rule of science. Alexander Pope's line in his *Essay on Man* — "God said, 'Let Newton be!' and all was light" — might well have been "God said 'Let Bacon be!' and all was light."

These features of Baconian science, however, also opened the door to the secularization of learning. Bacon depicted the relation of science and Christianity with an image of two books, the book

9. Bacon, *Novum Organum*, Aphorisms I.23ff.

of God's works and the book of God's word, both given us by God. He insisted these two books be studied separately, enjoining his readers not to "unwisely mingle or confound these learnings."[10] This may have been because he lived in troubled times when theology was a dangerous occupation, but other things also contributed to his desire to separate the two, including a more utilitarian view of learning, his acceptance of mechanistic rather than teleological science, a realignment of contemplation and action that excluded contemplation of eternal exemplars in God's mind, and a methodology that excluded religious presuppositions. Faith and learning could not therefore be integrated as they had been in the medieval university. The unity of truth (truths of revelation and truths of reason) no longer promised an integrated worldview; thanks to God's gift of reason and the order of his creation, science could do perfectly well alone. Religion was not relevant in doing science as such, but only in addressing conditions which make it possible and the ends to which it is devoted.

Bacon has become known for his dictum that "knowledge is power." He was sensitive to misuses of power, realizing that some people use it selfishly to extend their own power while some no less covetous use it to extend their country's power. He believed that others "more wholesome and noble," however, use knowledge to extend the power of the human race over nature. That is what he himself intended to do, and he wrote that we must use our knowledge in love, rather than for ostentation or "swelling of the head."[11] An ethic of power is at work here, one that sees life in the context of God's purposes for his creation. But a utilitarian view makes power (even if good uses of power) rather than wisdom and moral formation the goal for learning. Bacon's focus is

10. Bacon, *Advancement of Learning*, p. 179.
11. Bacon, *Novum Organum*, Aphorism II.129. See also his brief essay, "Of Goodness and Goodness of Nature," pp. 35-37.

on what one does with learning, rather than on the kind of person one becomes in the process. Even the wisdom he values in the study of history turns out to be the "what you can do with it" sort: don't study the thought of Augustine, he advises, as much as church history more generally, so as to see how people *used* what little they then knew. Bacon offers little but a consequentialist application of love. He summed up his ethic as did other nominalists of his day in the phrase "religion and right reason," which meant the Bible plus the ends it provided for utilitarian thinking. But secularized utilitarianism would be satisfied simply with ends we posit for ourselves, as has become evident since.

So did Bacon succeed in uniting contemplation and action more closely than before? He connects them by making the creation mandate and the relief of human need the means by which learning should glorify God. The connection is not intrinsic to the sciences involved, but extrinsic; not an internal relationship that flows from their very nature but something external to them, an overall "add on" intended by God. It is a kind of "value-added" education, in which the value of learning is in science's "practical" applications, not primarily in wisdom for its own sake, nor in transmitting a heritage of values that help shape character, nor in tracing the unity of truth and developing a world and life view. The focus is on what you can do with education in tangible, visible, this-life ways. It is not so much the liberal arts as the new mechanical arts, what we now know as technology and applied science, that are important, for that is where power is most evident. Bacon, of course, did not intend the wholly utilitarian approach to education that the Industrial Revolution introduced, but intended to combine the new science with an improved humanistic education, thereby wedding wisdom to scientific discovery.

In this regard he inspired English Puritan efforts at educational reform in the mid-seventeenth century. The Puritans similarly reacted not only against scholastic logic and meta-physics but also against classical humanism's overwhelming focus on classical languages and literature. More importantly, they saw connections between the educational system and existing economic, political, and social institutions, so that educational reform became part and parcel of the larger revolution they sought. Grandiose schemes were projected in which universal education for all social classes took the place of education intended only to produce "the complete gentleman" or to ensure a Bible-reading citizenry. The proposals emphasized utility, relevance, and experience, and were designed to improve the human condition. Ramist logic appealed because of its practicality, and Bacon's experiential approach to science resonated with the experiential emphasis in Puritan religion. The universities, however, served only the privileged, and even under Cromwell they remained a bastion of the ruling powers. Change came slowly. The Royal Society had been founded in 1622, but the new science remained outside the university until late in that century.[12]

Meanwhile Comenius, a Moravian bishop deeply influenced by Bacon, had spread the idea that teaching is itself a science. Moreover, since observation shows sense-knowledge to be the normal starting point for learning, abstract ideas should not be introduced until much later in the educational process. Comenius's "Pansophia" proposal sought harmony and peace through universal education, which would make available the totality of human knowledge. The Puritans too believed in the unity of knowledge; unlike Bacon, they countenanced no separation of religious knowledge from science, since the creator is revealed in nature, and they conceived of a massive system embracing

---

12. Richard L. Greaves, *The Puritan Revolt and Educational Thought* (New Brunswick, N.J.: Rutgers Univ. Press, 1969).

78

theology as well as the arts and sciences. Comenius's English translator and publisher, Samuel Hartlib, was also a Baconian who advocated an agricultural college and at one time wanted to replace scholastic divinity, law, and rhetoric with lectures on technology applicable to various trades. Comenius visited England in 1641; three years later John Milton dedicated his essay "On Education" to his friend and fellow Cambridge graduate, Samuel Hartlib.

Milton had been a voracious student. He traced his blindness, in fact, to having rarely quit his books before midnight ever since he was twelve. At Cambridge, however, he found the scholastic logic that dominated the curriculum "barren," so he extended his education independently into literature, history, philosophy, mathematics, and science. He was a Christian, a Baconian, and yet still a Renaissance humanist. As a Christian, he defined the goal of education thus:

> to repair the ruins of our first parents by regaining to know God aright, and out of that knowledge to love him, to imitate him, to be like him, as we may the nearest, by possessing our souls of true virtue, which being united to the heavenly grace of faith makes up the highest perfection.

As a Baconian he continued:

> But because our understanding cannot in this body found itself but on sensible things, nor arrive so clearly to the knowledge of God and things invisible, as by orderly conning over the visible and inferior creature, the same method is necessarily to be followed in all teaching.

The humanist who set forth the old cosmology in *Paradise Lost* nevertheless envisioned the complete gentleman as a practical man:

I call therefore a complete and generous education that which fits a man to perform justly, skillfully and magnanimously all the offices both private and public of peace and war.[13]

His specific proposals reflect this practicality. Mastery of one's own language is more important than classical languages: seven or eight years of early schooling in Latin and Greek provide little of practical use, only elegant maxims and Erasmus-like "copia." Even the children of gentry too soon spend an excessive amount of time on the abstractions of scholastic logic and metaphysics, while the law depends on long arguments and high fees instead of justice and prudence, and politics is conducted with clever adages and flattering speeches rather than with wisdom. People choose lives of luxury and ease.

Milton envisioned an education that would be both school and university for students from twelve to twenty-one years of age, a residential community educating the whole person through studies, exercise, and a healthy diet. The literature studied, he believed, should be both enjoyable and conducive to a love of virtue and work (a Reformed work ethic is plainly in mind), and classical writings about agriculture should provide an empirical starting point for the study of natural science. At the higher levels, poetry would be introduced, and ethics would include "the beginning, end and reason for political societies" and also the foundations of law in Moses as well as in Greece, Rome, and Saxon common law. Rhetoric and logic would come last, because students then could use them in refining thought and language in matters they had studied. As in classical rhetoric, students were to draw on a breadth of knowledge. In addition, physical exercise

13. "On Education," in *Complete Poetry and Selected Prose of John Milton* (New York: Modern Library, 1942).

would provide teaching opportunities in weaponry and observation of agriculture and commerce, while music with its influence over the emotions could contribute relaxation and refinement. This sort of education, he believed, would equip the young for life's responsibilities. As preparation for action rather than for contemplation, for work that serves society rather than for becoming social parasites, it reflects the goals of the Puritan revolution and the liberties it sought.

As a Puritan, Milton rejected the divine right of kings and disagreed with Thomas Hobbes's theory that the social contract gives rulers absolute authority. When parliament abolished censorship by the Star Chamber but talked instead of licensing the publication of books, he sent them a classical oration whose title recalls ancient Athens's freedom of speech. The *Areopagitica* began with a quotation from Euripides:

> This is true liberty, when free-born men
> Having to advise the public may speak free,
> Which he who can, and will, deserves high praise,
> Who neither can nor will may hold his peace;
> What can be juster in a state than this?[14]

He likened licensing to the Catholic Church's Index of forbidden books, "as if Peter bequeathed them the keys of the press also." Licensing could not prevent evil: a wise man like a good refiner will gather gold from the "drossiest" volume, but a fool will be a fool with the best book or none at all. Censorship would destroy all ability in disputation and thereby arrest the ongoing reformation of learning. It would be like homicide: while killing a man kills a rational being, destroying a good book kills reason itself, the image of God. In giving us reason God gave us choice, and

14. John Milton, *Areopagitica*, in *Selected Prose*, p. 677.

that is what is threatened. To believe something is true for no reason other than that the pastor says so borders on heresy. Faith and knowledge thrive on exercise, and given freedom of disputation truth will triumph over error. Freedom to learn, therefore, is essential for those "evidently born to study, who love learning for itself, for no other end than the service of God and of truth."[15]

This ideal of academic freedom is a corollary of Bacon's shift from education as the transmission of a heritage from the past to learning as the discovery of new knowledge. Bruce Kimball in fact sees two different conceptions of what "liberal" means in "liberal arts": learning appropriate to freemen (in Renaissance times "gentlemen of leisure") or freedom to learn without restraint, akin to freedom of speech and action.[16] In any case, nineteenth- and twentieth-century concepts of academic freedom often presuppose that learning and teaching should be as independent of outside influences as Bacon wanted science to be. But while the new science began to gain a place within the university late in the seventeenth century, Cambridge and Oxford continued in the scholastic and humanist traditions until the nineteenth century, and their influence was dominant in the American colonies, where colleges tended to combine classical humanism with religious education.

15. John Milton, *Areopagitica*, in *Complete Poetry and Selected Prose.*
16. Bruce A. Kimball, *Orators and Philosophers: A History of the Idea of Liberal Education* (New York: Teachers College Press, 1986), ch. 5.

EIGHT

Newman, the Liberal Arts, and Secularization

Beginning in the mid-nineteenth century, higher education in both Britain and America was profoundly affected by the Enlightenment and by its outcome in the Industrial Revolution. Both of these developments bore the marks of Bacon's scientific ideals, revealing on the one hand the secularizing influence of an inductive science independent of religious perspectives,[1] and on the other a more utilitarian approach to education. Opposing these tendencies at their beginning was an Oxford University teacher whom Jacques Barzun calls "the greatest theorist of university life," and whose classic work Jaroslav Pelikan acclaims as "the most important treatise on the idea of the university ever written in any language."[2]

---

1. See David Bebbington, "The Secularization of British Universities since the Mid-Nineteenth Century," in *The Secularization of the Academy,* ed. George Marsden and Bradley Longfield (New York: Oxford Univ. Press, 1992), p. 259; Marsden, *The Soul of the American University* (New York: Oxford Univ. Press, 1994).

2. Jaroslav Pelikan, *The Idea of a University: A Reexamination* (New Haven: Yale Univ. Press, 1992), pp. 6, 9.

John Henry Newman entered Trinity College, Oxford, as an undergraduate in 1816. An avid reader and painstaking student, he was disappointed by both the irresponsible lifestyle of his peers and the lack of academic guidance. The curriculum showed classical humanist influences but focused on a few required books and limited theological reading while largely ignoring more recent literature and science. It supposedly produced cultured gentlemen with social skills and leadership ability, but critics thought it more like an expensive club for changing boys into men. Intellectual development was not the essential point. Oriel College was something of an exception: a deeper seriousness of purpose was evident there, and a fellowship was offered on the basis of intellectual ability and originality rather than the technical expertise and bulk of knowledge more often expected. In 1822 Newman applied and was elected, and found the kind of intellectual community for which he longed. The Oriel common room was the essence of university life with its daily discussions about political, economic, and intellectual affairs, and, when he perceived that too many lectures seemed merely to recite facts, Newman proposed a student debating society to strengthen the education.[3]

He had been exposed to evangelical influences as a boy in boarding school and later recalled his religious conversion at the age of fifteen as the most momentous event in his entire life. But at Oriel he was increasingly attracted to the church fathers and the Anglican high-church tradition. He considered three possible ways of serving: as a college tutor, a parish priest, or a missionary to the heathen. For a short while he did serve as curate in a local parish, and the idea of serving in foreign missions appealed to

3. I am indebted to Dwight Culler, *The Imperial Intellect: A Study of Newman's Educational Ideal* (New Haven: Yale Univ. Press, 1955), and Ian Ker, *John Henry Newman: A Biography* (Oxford: Clarendon Press, 1988).

his wide intellectual interests, but he saw the tutor's role itself as a kind of pastoral care in the Greek *paedagogos* tradition, so he took a tutorial position at Alban Hall. There, in the face of irresponsible student escapades, he exercised strong discipline and urged more serious preparation for holy communion. At Oriel, where he became a tutor in 1826, he cultivated friendships with students that provided intellectual as well as moral and spiritual guidance. As a teacher he devised questions to make his students think for themselves, helping them to truly understand a book and discover its underlying assumptions, and he also set out to improve the college's tutorial system. Admissions qualifications were raised, written work was required in term finals, and the lecture system was reorganized to group better students in small sections with their own tutors.

Meanwhile, ten times a year the Church of St. Mary's invited selected clergy to deliver a University Sermon. Newman used these occasions to spell out principles basic to university education, such as the relationships between both faith and reason and reason and revelation, and the importance of moral and spiritual development. He was in fact working out the educational ideas he would later present in *The Idea of a University*.

Newman's was by no means the only voice, however. The Industrial Revolution was underway, and an Edinburgh review had lampooned undergraduate education in English universities as out of touch with reality and therefore unable to prepare students for the real world. This lack of practical usefulness was somewhat offset by the founding of Mechanics Institutes and the popular publications of The Society for the Diffusion of Useful Knowledge — useful, but unrelated to humanist learning or religious knowledge. In 1825 a university in London was proposed for the middle classes, one not like Oxford and Cambridge, but non-residential, non-sectarian, with no theological instruction, and without the costly tutorial system.

The colleges at Oxford and Cambridge were all related to the Church of England, with the result that dissenters and Roman Catholics were excluded. Newman opposed attempts to repeal this restriction, believing that to do so would destroy the pastoral role of tutors, prevent any required teaching of theology, and undermine church authority in both religious and civil affairs. He organized the opposition, helped launch the Tractarian campaign, and became the leading voice in the Oxford Movement. The proposed repeal failed.

The battle was over, but not the war. The basic issue that had aroused Newman's opposition was not just the call for useful knowledge or a broader admissions policy, but what he saw as Enlightenment liberalism intruding from politics into religion. Among the propositions he opposed were that no religious tenet is important unless reason shows it to be so, that no theological doctrine is anything more than an opinion which happens to be held by bodies of men, and that no revealed doctrine may reasonably stand in the way of scientific conclusions. The light of reason gives each individual the capacity to judge for himself, it was said, but Newman was convinced that individualism in the name of liberty extended the new freedom of scientific inquiry to all of life, submitting to the human mind what should rest simply on the authority of God's word.[4] Such an elevation of reason and individual preference made the individual sovereign and any creed as good as another; even dissenters seemed to him to follow nothing but personal preference. Tradition, the church fathers, and the authority of Scripture were all at stake, so he opposed liberalism in religion as a false liberty of thought, stressing the church's teaching authority instead, and he opposed liberalism in politics wherever it affected the church.

4. Newman, *Apologia Pro Vita Sua* (London: Longmans, Green, and Co., 1873), pp. 285-97.

Newman's emphasis on church tradition and authority eventually led him, in 1845, to embrace Catholicism. He therefore left Oxford and was shortly ordained as a Catholic priest, bringing years of experience to that tradition and educational ideals with wide appeal. His conversion to Catholicism coincided with a proposal by the British liberal government to establish a nonsectarian Queen's University in Ireland, since Dublin's Trinity College, like Oxford and Cambridge, admitted only Anglicans. The Catholic hierarchy was opposed to the project, and urged the establishment of a Catholic university instead. In 1851 Newman was approached about becoming the rector of this new Catholic institution. He served for seven years, the first three before the school actually began, during which time he delivered several of the lectures which were to comprise *The Idea of a University.*[5]

The university was to be a residential community, with tutors responsible for student development, religious and moral as well as intellectual. To that end, tutors were to maintain a structured and disciplined relationship with students, influencing them by the quality of their own lives. The institution began in a Georgian mansion in Dublin with twenty students, and the following year there were ninety-four; it continued throughout the nineteenth century and eventually became part of the National University of Ireland. Like medieval universities, it was to include schools of medicine, law, and "mechanics" as well as liberal arts, although Newman saw only the liberal arts and medicine come to fruition. He resigned in 1858 because of the pressures and difficulties of the task. As English gentry, he was ill prepared to understand and gain acceptance from the Irish, and their middle class could

5. All references will be to the 1960 Holt, Rinehart and Winston edition, edited by Martin Svaglic. The new 1996 Yale Univ. Press edition includes a series of helpful essays in addition to the main discourses, but only four of the original ten lectures on "University Subjects."

ill afford the expense. The bishops and priests wanted a younger and more vigorous Irish rector, and, since they disapproved of Newman's intention to draw students from places other than Ireland, it was difficult for him to secure sufficient numbers of students of reasonable caliber.

Newman's greatest and most lasting contributions were the discourses on educational philosophy and lectures on university subjects that make up *The Idea of a University*. There he argues both for liberal learning (as opposed to utilitarian education) and for the necessity of including theology rather than secularizing learning. That, of course, would require a different relationship of faith and reason than what was characteristic of Enlightenment science.

The university, he contends from the outset, is "a place of teaching universal knowledge," and knowledge is the expansion of intellect. What kind of university would best discipline the intellect: a non-residential one without tutorial supervision, that gives degrees to anyone passing a set range of examinations, or one with no professors and no examinations at all, which simply brings young men together for three or four years? Students in the latter alternative, Newman believes, are likely to have

> more thought, more mind, more philosophy, more true enlightenment, than those . . . who are forced to load their minds with a score of subjects against an examination, who have too much on hand to indulge themselves in thinking or investigation, who devour premises and conclusions together with indiscriminate greediness, who . . . when their period of education is passed, throw up all they have learned in disgust.[6]

It would be better to be an independent mind, roaming the library at random. Newman is plainly thinking of the Oriel com-

6. Newman, *The Idea of a University,* Discourse VI, pp. 112f.

mon room, where students and teachers represented the whole circle of liberal arts and learned to respect, consult, and help each other.

The knowledge he has in mind, then, is no passive recitation of subject matter but an active engagement that expands the mind, organizing and interpreting material, digesting it and making it subjectively one's own, and interrelating the old with the new within a comprehensive view of the whole world as the work of God. This habit of viewing objects in their larger context, what we call "worldview thinking," he calls "wisdom" or simply "philosophy." It is heart-searching in its knowledge of human nature, free from small-minded prejudice, but enriched with the contemplation of eternal order and beauty.[7] The doxological theme of monastery schools echoes loud and clear.

Newman is effusive about the intellectual virtues that result: force of mind, steadiness, versatility, good sense, reasonableness, command over one's own powers, and an instinctively just assessment of whatever transpires.

> To open the mind, to correct it, refine it, to enable it to know, and to digest, master, rule and use its knowledge, to give it power over its own faculties, application, flexibility, method, critical exactness, sagacity, resource, address, eloquent expression, is an object . . . as intelligible as the cultivation of virtue, while at the same time it is absolutely distinct from it.[8]

This is the self-rewarding nature of liberal learning that is useful in and of itself, independent of other ends. It needs no other

7. See Newman, *Idea,* Discourse VI; see also Sermon 14 in his *Fifteen Sermons Preached Before the University of Oxford Between* A.D. 1826 and 1843, ed. M. K. Tillman (Notre Dame, Ind.: Univ. of Notre Dame Press, 1997); also Culler, *The Imperial Intellect,* ch. 10.

8. Newman, *Idea,* Discourse V, p. 92.

end to make it worthwhile. Liberal knowledge is not useful merely by virtue of societal applications of science that are extrinsic to the science itself, but is intrinsically useful. For the utilitarians, education's benefits are extrinsic, in the practical usefulness of facts learned and skills acquired. While Newman was articulating his views in the 1850s, Charles Dickens's novel *Hard Times* appeared in periodical installments, lampooning the obsession with useful facts and the neglect of imagination, wonder, love, and moral development in Gradgrind's utilitarian school. The importance of persons was forgotten, Dickens claimed. Newman could not have agreed more.

Newman realized that Francis Bacon himself was not to blame; while an undergraduate he had acquired a twelve-volume set of Bacon's works and thus understood that the inductive method was not supposed to displace liberal studies or to secularize learning but was intended to improve physical and societal well-being. Newman calls Hobbes, Hume, and Bentham, however, "simply a disgrace," and he points an accusing finger at John Locke for limiting the value of education to its utility in a profession or trade while scorning both intellectual development undertaken for its own sake and the classical languages, for which a student will have no further use. Indeed, Locke wanted education "to produce virtuous, useful, and able young men in their distinct callings," and he regarded logic as helpful "for talk and opinion" but not "in the real performances of nature." Knowledge of the sciences, moreover, he considered "not necessary for a gentleman whose proper calling is service of his country"; the only necessity is what belongs to that calling.[9]

9. J. Adamson, ed., *Educational Writings of John Locke* (Cambridge: University Press, 1922), p. 24. See also "Some Thoughts Concerning Reading and Study for Gentlemen," *The Works of John Locke* (London, 1854), vol. II, pp. 497-504; and Newman's Lecture III on "English Catholic Literature," *Idea,* p. 238.

Newman agrees, of course, that the mere amassing of facts is not good education, but neither is the utilitarian approach. Knowledge is not just information, the *what* of learning, it is also the *how* (the intellectual activity of digesting facts, forming concepts, drawing inferences, and grounding them in first principles) and the *why* (the overall wisdom of a coherent worldview that relates knowledge to faith). Utilitarianism threatens both the *how* and the *why,* and Locke's fallacy is in supposing that no knowledge is useful that does not relate to an earthly calling or a mechanical act.

Premature specialization is also a mistake, if it separates various professions and fields of learning. It can degrade a rational being by narrowing his abilities and mental habits to what is useless elsewhere. The variety of callings needs some common link, a common cultural heritage with a common language and literature, if one is to be a friend, a companion, a citizen, a member of society, and not just a specialized professional. We need sufficient breadth of learning to catch the spirit behind the overall picture. Bacon said that history provided that fullness, that moral philosophy gives resolve, and that poetry elevates the understanding. Newman wants education that gives a clear and conscious view of one's own opinions and judgments, a grasp of their truth, eloquence in expressing them, and forcefulness in urging them. Such an education teaches a person "to see things as they are, to go right to the point, to disentangle a skein of thought, to detect sophistry and discard the irrelevant." It provides transferable skills applicable to any position, the ability to master any subject and understand what other people think. A person will know when to speak and when to be silent, will be able to converse, ask pertinent questions, or listen, because the mind lives "both in itself and in the world."[10] What is the chief

10. Newman, *Idea,* Discourse VII, p. 135.

end of man? That is the basic question, for whatever is that end is also the chief end of education. If it is more than the happiness and well-being that utilitarianism desires, then education has more than immediate, practical uses.

Liberal education, Newman recognizes, does not automatically and unambiguously support Christian belief, nor can it mend a sinful heart, but it might draw the mind away from harmful things, help build a conscience, and point to a divine lawgiver. Secular rationalism, on the other hand, reduces conscience to moral taste and makes us the lawgivers. It can harm revealed religion in two ways, by ignoring it and by adulterating it. Scientists who are only satisfied by laws of nature may ignore theology and resent religious interference, and literature portrays people in rebellion against God; yet theology offers a remedy for both. It completes a scientific explanation by revealing the final cause to whom nature leads, and it corrects the literary picture with remedies that grace supplies. Liberal learning without theology lacks the wisdom that comes from an overall vision, a worldview that unifies all branches of learning and elevates them to the contemplation of God.

His basic argument, then, is that the university is a place where universal knowledge is taught and so no part of it may be omitted. It is inconsistent to omit knowledge of the supreme being, whether that knowledge is drawn from reason or from revelation. Limiting learning to what sense experience teaches will exclude ethics, admitting moral experience will still omit history, allowing the evidence that supports history will still exclude metaphysics and abstract reasoning. The reality of God is supported by testimony handed down through history, inferred by inductive reasoning, brought home as a metaphysical necessity, and urged on us by moral conscience. The knowledge of God is therefore a subject on which all phenomena and all branches of learning converge, and theology itself is a science. Faith is not just subjective feeling or socially beneficial custom but an intellectual act that accepts revealed truth. If the object of knowledge is objective truth about facts and relationships, then universal knowledge, the knowledge of truth as a whole, is not possible without theology.

While he was working on these university lectures, Newman discovered that the *Edinburgh Encyclopaedia* of his day had articles on particular sciences but not on "science" as such, and none on "philosophy." It portrayed knowledge as an unconnected miscellany. Newman despised that picture as much as he did the student who amasses facts with no reason other than to pass examinations. Universal knowledge, for him, meant an integrally related system. He therefore contributed to Coleridge's abortive attempt to create an encyclopedia that would portray the unity of knowledge rather than merely contain a collection of mutually independent sciences, any of which could be omitted without changing the others. The omission of any one science prejudges the accuracy and completeness of others, for different sciences study different aspects of one and the same object: we study the human person as a physical being in the natural sciences, while psychology examines his mental makeup, sociology looks at relationships within the family and community, and theology views us in relationship to our Maker. These sciences influence each other, keeping us from reductionist accounts and providing a more interrelated picture. Newman therefore claims that we cannot teach any one science thoroughly unless all the related sciences, including theology, are taken into account. Theology is not just part of knowledge but the condition of it and the subject on which they all converge, so that omitting it is like omitting the principal part from a drama. He speaks of "the imperial intellect" (using the analogy of the British Empire of his day) according to which theology is the queen of the sciences, the science of all other disciplines, the overarching context that integrates sciences and humanities in relation to God and his purposes for church and society.[11]

Newman recognized that this unity of truth was largely lost in his day. Francis Bacon had led positivists like Auguste Comte and Jeremy Bentham to think that inductive methods are what unify the sciences, with the result that theology and metaphysics were systematically excluded. The resultant lack of systemic unity encouraged specialization, which fragmented learning and opened the way to reductionist explanations that ignored the multiplicity of causes, both natural and divine.

There might be no need for a Catholic Euclid or Newton, Newman conceded, since natural science is objective, the same for everyone. But the arts, he believed, were different, so he urged the development of Catholic literature, not necessarily religious literature as such but writings that would treat any and every subject as only Catholics can: novels, for instance, that introduce grace into the picture of human fallenness, and works that ground social ideals in theology or put them to work in politics and economics.[12]

Growing conflicts between science and religion made the Irish bishops uneasy with Newman's intellectual emphasis, but Newman blamed these conflicts on each of the disciplines encroaching on the other's territory, a practice he thought quite unnecessary. Since science and theology have different methods and different subject matter, they cannot really touch each other. Physical science deals with facts, theology with reasons for them; the sciences are inductive, theology deductive; physics treats efficient causes, theology final causes; physics seeks natural laws, theology the lawgiver, but both believe in fixed natural laws. If

11. Discourses II, III, and IV of Newman's *Idea* address this. See also Culler, *The Imperial Intellect,* ch. 9.

12. Newman, Lecture III, "English Catholic Literature," in *Idea,* p. 221.

truth is ultimately one, then truth in one field may *seem* to, but really cannot, contradict truth in another. We simply need to define their respective territories.

The scientist need not always collide with theological truth, trespass into biblical interpretation, or otherwise scandalize those weak in the faith. But great minds nevertheless need elbow room, so when apparent conflicts arise the scientist need not continually adjust his course to fit other disciplines, but should keep investigating within his own science. Doing science takes character: earnestness in the pursuit of truth rather than self-gratification, patience and modesty in reaching conclusions rather than rash assertions, and a cooperative spirit are required.[13]

Yet, if all truth is one, are the disciplines really so separate? On the one hand, Newman says, yes, but on the other he claims that each discipline is influenced by the presence of others. The question must then be asked, can scientists be prevented from voicing theological questions, or theologians from criticizing some scientific theory? Is natural science as purely inductive, objective, and universally agreed on as Newman assumes? In fact, Bacon's separation of science and theology fractured the systematic unity of knowledge, much as Abelard's Aristotelian logic had fractured the unity of knowledge in his day. In this regard, Newman was in a similar predicament to the Scottish realists in American higher education, but they extended the use of the inductive method into theology and added a moral philosophy course without challenging the Enlightenment frame of mind.

Newman, however, was less concerned about science than about other aspects of the faith and reason relationship. His Oxford Movement, which had begun as a protest against the ratio-

13. Newman, Lecture VII, "Christianity and Physical Science," in *Idea,* p. 321; and Culler, *The Imperial Intellect,* ch. 13.

nalistic tendency of the universities, provided a theological voice for a more romanticist view of nature. This view saw nature not as dead and exploitable but as an imaginative divine language, in that respect echoing medieval symbolists like Bonaventure and doing for England the kind of thing Schleiermacher had done for Germany. Like Jonathan Edwards he emphasized the affections as well as the intellect, for he saw a teleology in human nature that disposes the whole person to faith. Like Augustine he realized that "our hearts are restless until they rest in God."

This, in part, is why he so valued the study of literature: it speaks to the imagination. He himself wrote poetry as well as theology and philosophy, and his novel *Callista*[14] recounts the conversion of a young, third-century woman who was martyred. Her life was empty, without meaning or purpose, and a deep hunger and thirst gnawed at her heart. Her needs, desires, and aspirations all called for something to love. This emptiness defined her whole life: as she put it, "you cannot escape yourself." It demanded a real object of love, but she could not conceive what such an ideal object could be. Her servant was a Christian, but she herself thought Christianity too beautiful to be anything but imagination, a dream. Its Loved One was merely an ideal, not a reality, and its view of a new community of people was too good to be true — yet it told of a higher beauty than the order and harmony that nature revealed. Gradually she saw the plausibility of its doctrine, and the more she heard of Christianity, the more she was drawn to it and the more it responded to her every need. She was captivated by reading Luke's Gospel, for it spoke to her conscience like the echo of a person's voice, as if the one she was seeking was indeed real.

Newman's concept of conscience is the key to this story of faith and knowledge. More than moral awareness, and certainly

14. First published in 1856. Sheed and Ward, 1941.

more than social conditioning, it is the inner voice of human needs, hopes, and aspirations, evoking the sense of an ideal person, one solely good, whom we should love. Christianity appeals to the imagination because the conscience recognizes the antecedent probability that such a person must really exist. Faith is not the result of unimpassioned intellectual inquiry, dependent on logical arguments or inductive probabilities, but a more holistic response to Christ. It is true that the intellect is involved; Callista, for example, saw the plausibility of Christian doctrine and felt the force of arguments to which she previously was an utter stranger. Her friend Agellius had explored various religions and philosophies, understood how they regarded Christianity, and knew something about its intellectual justification. He knew also that for Christians, certain inclinations and rules become matters of conscience, first principles that govern both life and thought. Nevertheless, what eventually brought him to faith was the love of Christ he saw through believers like Callista who were faithful in the face of death.

Newman had developed this view of the relation between reason, the passions, and faith in his University Sermons preached years before at St. Mary's Church.[15] Conscience attests to ideals rooted in our very nature, ideals we contemplate but, at the cost of real happiness, fail to attain. Conscience cannot move the heart to love the good, and it cannot make us truly virtuous. Nor can it prove its own authority, for natural religion alone is not persuasive. It may point to a divine moral governance, but not to the more personal divine attributes that elicit loving obedience. Only revealed religion can supply that, for only Christ the Incarnate Word, Light, Wisdom, and Truth embodies in human nature all the ideals conscience can imagine. He is the ideal object of our faith and love.

15. Newman, Sermons 2 and 3 in *Fifteen Sermons*.

What place has reason, then, in faith development? At best, it is an instrument in the hands of spiritual development. Conscience produces moral convictions, and moral convictions make implicit assumptions about an ideal object, assumptions which tacit reasoning uses as informal premises for religious inquiry. So, while faith is not necessarily founded on explicit reasoning, reason may still explore Christian evidence, interpret Scripture, or decide a question about faith and morals. These rational considerations gradually converge on a conclusion that is credible and real to the imagination, with a certitude that goes beyond dispassionate probability to wholehearted assent.

While still at Oriel, Newman observed that when the Reformation broke with the church's authority, "reason" volunteered its proofs.[16] He therefore warns that the reasoning of secular minds is (1) explicit, (2) evidentialist, and (3) based on secular assumptions that color and interpret the evidence. Such reasoning does not correct its own theological mistakes, but usurps the church's authority as "the pillar and ground of truth." It had become, Newman believed, a *sine qua non* for religious faith, and against this development Newman argued vigorously. Mere evidence leads to passive belief, but faith does not always allow time for minute and finished investigation. It is "the substance of things hoped for," based not on reason but on love. What then keeps it from ungrounded credulity and superstition? Love. The safeguard is a right state of heart: holiness, dutifulness, a new creation, right faith, the faith of a right mind formed by love for the Good. The corollary is clear. It is not reason, evidence, or logical skills that will lead students to the truth, but the moral power inherent in the personal influence of faithful mentors who model the character of the Christ they serve.

Newman developed his view of faith and reason most system-

16. Newman, Sermon 4 in *Fifteen Sermons*.

atically in *An Essay in Aid of a Grammar of Assent*.[17] John Locke had defined faith as assent to a proposition on the authority of divine revelation rather than on reason alone, and had claimed that assent should be proportioned to the evidence. But since evidence is a matter of degrees, faith also is a matter of degrees. Newman objects that Locke has confused assent with inference: inference differs from assent in the same way that assessing subjective ideas differs from apprehending reality. The one is just an intellectual process, the other a real action in a real world. A child's assent to the veracity and authority of her mother is not just an abstract idea, but is bound up with the child's image and love of her: it is part of the child's very being. And the more the experience of mother occupies her, the keener will be the assent. There may be degrees of assent, but not in proportion to evidence and argument alone. Logicians are more set on concluding rightly (with valid logic) than they are concerned with right conclusions. But there is no end of logical argument and counter-argument unless we start from first principles rooted in the realities of concrete experience. The certainty logic seeks is just an intellectual thing, a property of propositions, while the certitude in real assent is a mental state that actively embraces the reality it represents. It is a natural condition developed by natural pro-

17. Longmans, Green, and Co., 1930 (1st publ. 1870). With recent reactions against Enlightenment epistemology, a considerable body of literature has developed on his theory of conscience and imagination. See Gerald Casey, *Natural Reason: A Study of the Notions of Inference, Assent, Intuition, and First Principles in the Philosophy of John Henry Cardinal Newman* (New York: Peter Lang, 1984); John Coulson, *Reason and Imagination: "in Aid of a Grammar of Assent"* (Oxford: Clarendon Press, 1981); M. Jamie Ferreia, *Scepticism and Reasonable Doubt: The British Naturalist Tradition in Wilkins, Hume, Reid, and Newman* (Oxford: Clarendon Press, 1986); William Wainwright, *Reason and the Heart: A Prolegomenon to a Critique of Passional Reason* (Ithaca: Cornell Univ. Press, 1995).

cesses in the course of life: it can grow and endure without explicit inferences and arguments, and it can die while the reasons for it remain strong. This is the very nature of assent. And, as Callista said, we cannot deny our own nature.

Locke tried to impose his logical ideal on human nature, but human nature is too strong for Locke's ideal to be carried out in practice. Assent does not normally result from disinterested analysis but from what Newman calls the "illative sense" that evaluates evidence in the light of one's deepest convictions and aspirations. On the basis of these tacit first principles it recognizes when lines of converging probabilities are sufficient. This is an acquired habit originating in our nature but shaped and matured by practice and experience. It is similar to what we call "good sense," to Aristotle's practical wisdom (*phronesis*), or to Scottish Realism's "common sense," a created teleology for life in this world.

How does this view of faith and reason affect higher education? It challenges the Enlightenment's secularizing ideal of purely objective and disinterested knowledge available independent of other than purely intellectual interests. By doing so, it points to more holistic dimensions of the student mind, and so to the Augustinian ideal of an understanding that is faith's reward. Intellectual inquiry must go hand in hand with faith development and moral development if education is to shape the person as a whole.

NINE

The Christian Academy
in the Twentieth Century

Fallout from the Enlightenment continued throughout the nineteenth and twentieth centuries, and Newman's idea of a Christian university geared to classical humanism was but one response to liberal theology and the growing secularism. In 1879 the Papal encyclical *Aeternae Patris* called Catholic scholars to explore the resources of Thomas Aquinas in addressing the problems of modernity, for Aquinas taught that faith frees reason, saves it from error, and enriches it with new knowledge. For the next seventy-five years, neo-scholasticism shaped much of Catholic higher education, uniting faith with learning in the manner of pre-Enlightenment times. Much of the credit belongs to the Jesuits, the scholarly order founded by Ignatius Loyola in the sixteenth century. Their curriculum was traditional scholasticism. At Boston College as late as the 1950s, for instance, undergraduates took ten philosophy courses, including logic, metaphysics, natural theology, and ethics — quite a contrast to nearby Harvard's unpatterned elective system and to the European single-discipline education. But it brought together all that students learned into an orderly worldview.[1]

Some American Protestant colleges turned to the Scottish commonsense philosophy brought to Princeton by John Witherspoon, and followed its assumption that our God-given faculties provide reliable knowledge. It was not the Enlightenment ideal of objective and universal knowledge that they opposed but its agnostic outcomes. Rejecting Locke's theory of subjective ideas in favor of direct realism, they adopted an empirically based apologetic and capstoned collegiate education with a moral philosophy course that taught personal and social responsibility in the context of a Christian worldview. At Wheaton College this kind of approach continued until the mid-twentieth century.

Protestantism had no scholarly order like the Jesuits, but in 1944, as Europe faced the task of re-educating a world ravaged by ideological barbarism, Arnold Nash envisioned a worldwide order of Christian scholars with a fourfold task:

1. To discover an answer not only to the question "How can we as individuals serve God in the university?" but also to the question "How can the liberal democratic university itself be a witness to the glory of God?"
2. To discover the meaning of a Christian vocation for a man or woman who is a chemist, sociologist, historian, psychologist, mathematician, and the like.
3. To apply Christian criteria in working out the presuppositions which are relevant to the study of individual academic

---

1. James Burtchaell, *The Dying of the Light* (Grand Rapids: Eerdmans, 1998), p. 577. On Catholic Higher Education see Philip Gleason, *Contending with Modernity: Catholic Higher Education in the Twentieth Century* (New York: Oxford Univ. Press, 1995).

subjects, and to discover the place in a Christian *speculum mentis* of the knowledge given in such specialized subjects.

4. To work toward an intellectual synthesis for the twentieth century which, as an interpretation of human life and destiny, can be set over against the positivistic, the Marxist, the liberal humanitarian *Weltanschauungen* now current in the liberal democratic world. . . . Like Scholasticism, it will derive unity from its theological basis which will provide its presuppositions.[2]

Sir Walter Moberly observed in 1949 that scientific humanism rather than Christianity had become the major influence, so that the university now gave itself to research more than to teaching, and did so for learning's sake rather than for the sake of student formation. Learning was fragmented, while foundational and ethical issues were largely ignored with a false air of neutrality and irresponsible detachment. Underscoring the importance of a teacher's overall worldview, he called for a return to the Christian tradition.[3]

About the same time, C. S. Lewis published *The Abolition of Man*, a work about a writing textbook whose rules allowed only statements of observable facts and treated value judgments as merely subjective feelings. This was a tragic mistake, Lewis argued, for it effectively makes us "men without chests," with intellect and feeling but no capacity to love, no ideals to cherish, nothing to live for, no real humanity. It exposed the educational outcome of secularization in the positivism of that day.

2. Arnold Nash, *The University and the Modern World: An Essay in the Social Philosophy of University Education* (London: S.C.M. Press, 1945), p. 205.

3. Sir Walter Moberly, *The Crisis in the University* (London: S.C.M. Press, 1949). Fifty years later Warren Nord and Charles Haynes protested the legally unnecessary exclusion of religious studies from American public education in *Taking Religion Seriously Across the Curriculum* (Alexandria, Va.: First Amendment Center, 1998).

In America, meanwhile, *The Christian Scholar* discussed the theological foundations of Christian higher education, encouraging teachers to uncover worldviews and hidden assumptions and to develop Christian perspectives in their disciplines. The existential theology then current, however, could not effectively overcome the positivist separation of objectively scientific facts from religious beliefs and values, with the result, as Douglas Sloan has shown, that mainline Protestantism settled for a dualistic approach rather than attempting to integrate faith and learning.[4]

A more effective response to secularized thinking, one that denies the Enlightenment ideal of autonomous reason and recalls Augustine's "faith seeking understanding," came from Reformed scholars. The Dutch theologian Abraham Kuyper, in his 1898 Stone lectures at Princeton University, spoke of Calvinism as a "life system" or worldview in conflict with modern naturalism and its implications in religion, politics, science, and art.[5] "Calvinism," as he used the term, referred not to a particular theology but to the central Christian conviction that the entire universe and all of life belong to Christ, and that it is from this conviction that thought and action must begin. This means that there are two kinds of people, those who confess Christ as Lord and those who do not, and therefore two kinds of life systems and two kinds of science exist as well. A worldview is not primarily a theoretical scheme but a pre-theoretical perspective stemming from "the

4. See *The Christian Scholar,* vol. 11 (Aug. 1958), a publication of the Commission on Higher Education of the National Council of Churches; Douglas Sloan, *Faith and Knowledge: Mainline Protestantism and American Higher Education* (Louisville: Westminster John Knox Press, 1994).

5. Abraham Kuyper, *Lectures on Calvinism* (Grand Rapids: Eerdmans, 1931). See also Kuyper's *Principles of Sacred Theology,* trans. J. Hendrick de Vries (New York: Charles Scribner's Sons, 1898), second division, ch. 2 and 3.

deepest impulse of each life consciousness." The theological and philosophical foundations of academic disciplines and professional practice are therefore critical, and the conflict with modern naturalism must be addressed accordingly. Kuyper thus spoke about "science and sin," referring not simply to falsehood but to unintentional mistakes, self-deception, faulty imagination, misleading language habits, and disorganized relationships with colleagues. Nevertheless, science is made possible by the law-structure God created, which is accessible to all regardless of differing worldviews, so that broad areas of agreement are possible between Christian and non-Christian scientists. It is at the foundational level that worldview conflicts occur, and it is there that Christian scholarship must confront secularism.

In effect, Kuyper anticipated the postmodern reaction against Enlightenment thinking, for plainly no one worldview had gained the universal acceptance that knowledge was supposed to afford. In the 1950s in his landmark work, *The Structure of Scientific Revolutions*, Thomas Kuhn challenged the idea of a wholly objective science by tracing the influence of subjective, non-empirical factors in historical paradigm shifts. In the meantime, while Enlightenment individualism had given freedom to think independently, free of the constraints of any authority or tradition, now increased awareness of ethnic and gender differences revealed psychological and cultural influences in how we perceive and learn. The resultant pluralism has made the Enlightenment ideal of objective and universal knowledge seem impossible.

This should not surprise us if we take human finiteness seriously, for knowing is historically situated within the perspective of particular times and places. We gain confidence in our perceptions when they recur again and again and when others with different perspectives agree, for that is what careful science and honest discussion afford. But pluralism persists in differing moral and religious traditions and incompatible worldviews.

A more extreme postmodernism therefore concluded that not only knowledge but truth itself is relative, that objective truth does not exist. As Allan Bloom remarked, students talk as if there is no such thing as truth or falsity, no right or wrong; they have no worldview to ground such ideas, and no sense of personal identity.[6] There is no "big picture," no "metanarrative."

Such a view does not logically follow from the perspectival nature of human knowledge, however. Individual and cultural differences do not tell the whole story, for "perspective" also has generic human dimensions: common experiences, common needs and problems, common kinds of value. Scottish realism was right in this regard, that insofar as we are all alike we naturally tend to see things alike. We accept, for example, the existence of an external world with predictable processes and of other persons more or less like ourselves, and this testifies to the objectivity of truth. Human knowledge may be more or less perspectival, but not things in themselves, nor the truth about what they are, a truth which exists independent of whether we know it or not. Different worldviews may represent different perspectives on life, but this does not logically imply that metanarratives are no longer possible.

Long before the Enlightenment and postmodernity, Christian theology taught that God created in wisdom, with archetypal ideas in mind, that truth exists in God's own knowledge and is revealed in his creation. This is part of the metanarrative about Jesus Christ, the Logos of creation and redemption, and his kingdom that awaits fulfillment. It means that truth comes ultimately from God, no matter by what divinely provided means it is discovered. It gives epistemic confidence, confidence in the

6. Allan Bloom, *The Closing of the American Mind: How Higher Education Has Failed Democracy and Impoverished the Souls of Today's Students* (New York: Simon and Schuster, 1987).

existence of truth and confidence in reason as well as revelation. Epistemic modesty is important, to be sure, because of finiteness and sin, but epistemic confidence is needed in facing postmodernity. Carl Henry observes that the loss of God as Logos clouded the bond of intelligibility between man and nature, subordinating a supposedly unintelligible cosmos to man as intellectual voyager. He quotes fellow-theologian Langdon Gilkey: "the lack of religious faith in the Logos made flesh is balanced in our time by the lack of philosophical faith in the universal Logos in reality."[7]

Higher education has also been affected by the emphasis on specialized research, for specialization fragments learning, largely ignoring the unity of truth. Mark Schwehn complains that research universities changed the meaning of an academic vocation and that, by socializing graduate students into making research rather than teaching and student formation primary, they have contributed to the secularization of higher education.[8] The technological revolution has had a similar effect, and it strengthens the utilitarian approach to education. Technology itself may be largely value-free, but without any larger context it ignores questions about purpose and meaning and feeds the positivist schism between facts and values. As Albert Speer, Hitler's Minister of Munitions, reportedly observed after twenty-seven years in prison,

People who ask what "practical" purpose there is for studying subjects like history and philosophy need to be reminded that they are the only subjects that ask fundamental ques-

---

7. C. F. H. Henry, *God, Revelation and Authority*, vol. III (Waco, Tex.: Word Books, 1979), pp. 169, 202.

8. Mark Schwehn, *Exiles from Eden: Religion and the Academic Vocation in America* (New York: Oxford Univ. Press, 1993), ch. 1.

tions — What is the nature of man? What is the good society? What are the proper ends of civilization? and so forth.

One commentator added that the Germans were the most educated nation in the world, in the narrow sense of scholarship and technical skills, but that this was not translated by their academic system into ethical terms.

At stake in technological development is the very meaning of the human person, and Pope John Paul II therefore urges universities to stress "the priority of the ethical over the technical" and "the primacy of the person over things."[9] The claim I heard one famous scientist make, that technology can solve all of our problems, is flawed. From a biblical perspective it is heretical, even idolatrous. Clearly, a technological society needs broader understanding and the wisdom of both liberal learning and the Christian Scriptures. They are essential for the thinking a technological society needs, as well as for giving substance to a Christian worldview.

In this historical setting — secularized, technological, postmodern, multicultural — how relevant are the four historic concerns of Christians in higher education? Is a liberal arts education (to take the first concern) still useful preparation for service, whether professional or in a voluntary capacity, in church and society? I say "for service" rather than "for career preparation" because the Christian view of work as stewardship of the creation and service to others should inform how one earns a living or chooses a career. Such an understanding of the meaning and purpose of work is in fact a major benefit of liberal learning. Internships and service learning opportunities can reinforce such an understanding, since preparation and debriefing is in-

9. *On Catholic Universities: Ex Corde Ecclesiae* (U.S. Catholic Conference, 1990), p. 17.

tended to link theory with practice and classroom with workplace. (Student extracurricular projects in the community can have similar benefits.) Liberal education also facilitates understanding and effective communication across generations and cultures, while providing a common body of knowledge that remains open-ended. It broadens horizons, deepens understanding, cultivates new appreciations, and humanizes people who might otherwise be confined, narrow functionaries in the workplace. It is excellent career preparation because it educates the person, providing transferable skills and a knowledge of the disciplines on which professions and businesses are built.

Consider these useful contributions:

1. Breadth of learning gives access to the wealth of human learning and to the diversity of human experience.
2. Transferable skills (verbal, analytic, quantitative, communication, and social skills) are applicable to any kind of work; they facilitate lifetime learning and job mobility.
3. Historical and conceptual contexts interrelate the particulars of experience and enable one to uncover assumptions and underlying worldviews.
4. Engagement with moral values and social issues sensitizes and informs the conscience and contributes to character development.
5. Aesthetic experience nurtures and refines the imagination and develops an appreciation of beauty.
6. Holistic personal development — intellectual, cultural, moral, and spiritual — results.

Transferable skills are perhaps the greatest practical asset of an education in the liberal arts. The ability to think for oneself, to understand where someone else is coming from, and to uncover assumptions and see where a line of thought leads; to state oneself with clarity, precision, and grace; to sort out complexities in a problem, formulate alternative game plans, and discuss them without either seeming threatening or feeling threatened — these apply in any occupation. We need to cultivate a campus climate like Oriel's common room in Newman's day, where breadth of learning and the creative ferment of cross-disciplinary discussion about the major problems of the day flourish, where sloppy language and unthinking minds straighten up to meet higher levels of expectation.

Whether or not liberal arts education is regarded as useful will depend, of course, on what ends one has in mind. *The New York Times* recently published an article on the rising cost of a college education, suggesting that "one star academic beamed in via the internet" could replace hundreds of professors in their classrooms — as if the purpose of education is only to impart information. But novelist Gail Godwin cites a different school prospectus:

> Young people aren't being given the necessary minimum of intangibles to grow on. They suffer from psychic undernourishment. Wisdom is developed in young brains by the curriculum of conversation, thought, imagination, empathy and reflection. Young people need to generate language and ideas, not just listen and watch as passive consumers. At Fair Haven, we attempt to build a type of intelligence that is joyously able to contemplate a wide range of things, not simply for "career goals" but out of the mind's affection for its own proper objects. We also strive to restore the endangered virtues of kindness, introspection, and disinterested love: doing things not for gain, but because they are there to be done.[10]

10. Gail Godwin, *Evensong* (New York: Ballantine Books, 1999), p. 48.

Christopher Derrick warns that liberal education will prove insufficient and directionless unless it can presuppose a religion or at least some plausible philosophy of life.[11] This is especially the case with today's technological mentality, according to which if something is possible it must be done. Our increasingly secular technological society leaves larger questions unanswered — moral questions about how technology is used and to what ends, and questions about how it affects people and the human quality of the workplace and whether it dehumanizes relationships, alienates us from our inner selves, or threatens the environment. These are perennial concerns that aroused the ancient Cynics, and more recently the Marxists, existentialists, and simple-lifestyle advocates. We dare not ignore them in the twenty-first century.

Neither should we ignore an emphasis on moral and spiritual formation and care of the soul, the second of the traditional concerns of Christian education. Augustine's advice about a well-ordered student lifestyle was echoed in America until after World War II by *in loco parentis* campus rules, but the teacher's role as *paedagogos* has now been forgotten in the research-oriented conception of academic vocation. What then is left of student formation? Lamenting what they call the abandoned generation, two Duke University professors recommend developing small communities on campuses where students could find identity and be accountable.[12] Church-related institutions may seem to have a distinct advantage by virtue of their connection with historically continuous Christian communities, but James Burtchaell has

11. Christopher Derrick, *Escape from Scepticism: Liberal Education as if Truth Mattered* (LaSalle, Ill.: Sherwood Sugden & Co., 1977), p. 21.

12. William Willimon and Thomas Naylor, *The Abandoned Generation: Rethinking Higher Education* (Grand Rapids: Eerdmans, 1995). David Hoekema comes to similar conclusions in *Campus Rules and Moral Community: In Place of In Loco Parentis* (Lanham, Md.: Rowman and Littlefield, 1994).

painstakingly documented the disengagement of many colleges and universities from their sponsoring churches of whatever denomination. The vital theological reflection involved in denominational life, he believes, is needed to sustain the religious character of a college. It affects student formation because piety, morality, and theology are so closely connected that no one of the three has much stability without the others.[13]

Steven Garber draws similar conclusions from his study of mature Christian graduates who, over the years, have integrated belief with behavior. What that kind of integrity requires, he finds, is threefold: *convictions* (a worldview sufficient for life's questions and crises); *character* (a mentor who incarnates that worldview); and *community* (living out that worldview in company with mutually committed and stimulating people).[14]

Belief in the importance of moral exemplars and of community is now almost commonplace. Alasdair MacIntyre argues that worldview differences preclude any overall moral ideal common to all, so that in reality a particular morality is part of an ongoing historical tradition embodied in some community.[15] Christian morality is no exception, and it is by identifying with some Christian community and making its story and values one's own that character is naturally formed. Its moral heritage, proverbial wisdom, and moral exemplars create levels of expectation and a sense of accountability. The Greeks passed the wisdom of their community to new generations through the educational process. Solomon presented his proverbs as parental instruction to a family

---

13. Burtchaell, *The Dying of the Light,* ch. 8.

14. Steven Garber, *The Fabric of Faithfulness: Weaving Together Belief and Behavior During the University Years* (Downers Grove, Ill.: InterVarsity Press, 1996).

15. See especially *Three Rival Versions of Moral Enquiry* (Notre Dame, Ind.: Univ. of Notre Press, 1990).

for attaining wisdom and discipline;
    for understanding words of insight;
for acquiring a disciplined and prudent life,
    doing what is right and just and fair;
for giving prudence to the simple,
    knowledge and discretion to the young —
let the wise listen and add to their learning,
    and let the discerning get guidance. . . .

(Prov. 1:2-5)

It is wisdom, not just knowledge as Bacon claimed, that has power (Prov. 8:12-16).

Well-formed character is an integrated moral identity, the same day after day, the same inwardly and outwardly — not just a motley array of actions and behaviors or of good intentions and dispositions that never get implemented, but the integration of life by some unifying virtue that draws everything into harmony. Says Solomon, "The fear of the Lord is the beginning of wisdom" and "to fear the Lord is to hate evil" (Prov. 1:7; 8:13). Augustine's *Confessions* related his own moral and intellectual pilgrimage to his restless longing for God, anticipating the medieval linkage of a love of learning and the desire for God. Hugh of St. Victor linked *cogitatio* (disciplined thinking) and *meditatio* (moral self-scrutiny) in preparation for contemplating God. It remains the case today that moral, intellectual, and faith development are interconnected in a life integrated by love for God.

The integration of faith and learning ("reintegration" may be more appropriate in our secularized culture) involves far more than the conjunction of liberal learning and student formation. The unity of truth (our third traditional concern) in the mind of an all-knowing creator underlies the reintegration of Christian beliefs with the foundations, the content, and the practice of ac-

113

ademic disciplines. Christian beliefs provide theological foundations for knowledge and art, they reintroduce truths that would otherwise be ignored, and they give coherence to a worldview. This is not just a Reformed emphasis, for it reaches back through history to Augustine and the Alexandrians. That all truth is God's truth is a truism that all Christian traditions can appreciate. Mennonite institutions are likely to stress service learning, peace and reconciliation, and Third-World studies, for example, but this by no means precludes worldview thinking. Indeed, it presupposes it, for it is the Mennonite worldview that requires useful learning and a life of service. In H. Richard Niebuhr's *Christ and Culture,* on the other hand, Catholicism represents "Christ above culture," an image that reflects the medieval hierarchy of being in which liberal learning led to the contemplation of the eternal and of God. Nevertheless, Pope John Paul II recently advised university teachers to "set the content, objectives, methods and results of their research within the framework of a coherent world vision" and urged "a Christian spirit of service to others for the promotion of social justice."[16] Richard Neuhaus has written that

> it is within the Christian understanding of reality that everything finds its role, nothing that is true or good or beautiful can be excluded. . . .
>
> A Christian university has as its premise the knowledge that all truth is one and all ways to truth are one because the Author and the End of truth is One. . . .
>
> A Christian university will settle for nothing less than a comprehensive account of reality. Not content with the *what* of things, it wrestles with the *why* of things; not content with

16. *On Catholic Universities: Ex Corde Ecclesiae,* p. 19. See also Pope John Paul's encyclical, *Fides et Ratio* (Boston: Pauline Books and Media, 1998).

knowing *how,* it asks *what for.* Unlike other kinds of universities, the Christian university cannot evade the hard questions about what it all means. Therefore theology and philosophy, the sciences of meaning, are at the heart of the Christian university.[17]

Lutheran higher education, however, stresses a dialectical relationship between faith and learning. Unresolved and often unrecognized tensions between reason and revelation persist, making the unity of knowledge an impossible goal. According to one Lutheran scholar, education is a secular calling guided by reason, and no substantive difference may exist between scholarship by Christians and that by non-Christians. The Christian dimension is in the sense of calling and in the institutional context surrounding an academic enterprise.[18] If reason is presuppositionless factual thinking, as the Lutheran nominalist heritage assumed, this may well be the case. But postmodernism has called that kind of objectivity into question. Moreover, although foundational questions as well as a range of agreements and disagreements between faith and learning remain — for it is true that tensions persist and integration remains a lifelong task completely achieved only by God — the hope persists that some of these tensions can be resolved. The unity of knowledge is at best an ideal, and integration an unending task, but it is nonetheless implicit in the theological conviction that truth is one coherent whole in the omniscient mind of God.

The fourth and final traditional concern of the Christian

17. Richard Neuhaus, "The Christian University: Eleven Theses," *First Things*, Jan. 1996, pp. 20-22.

18. Mark U. Edwards, "Christian Colleges: A Dying Light or a New Refraction?," *Christian Century*, 21-28 April 1999, pp. 459-63.

academy is, as we have seen, a concern for contemplative or doxological learning. The doxological emphasis of the Middle Ages was tied to the contemplation of archetypal forms underlying the liberal arts, for Augustine had considered Plato's forms to be God's ideas, archetypes of things he could create. But "archetypes" does not necessarily mean Plato's universals, since John Calvin, Francis Bacon, and John Locke all use the term for God's ideas about what he would create. Twentieth-century doxologies arise instead from contemplating the intricate order and awesome grandeur of creation itself, from enjoying its bounty and beauty, from discovering great minds and wonderful new ideas. If the heavens declare the glory of God and the firmament shows his handiwork, or if we wonder that God so gifts his creatures, then liberal learning can still become a call to worship. It will be a holistic kind of spirituality — not a compartmentalized piety, peripheral or even opposed to rigorous academics, but one that heartily embraces all of learning and life and delights in every indication of God's wisdom, goodness, and power. Contemplation (*contemplatio*) was not analytic thinking (*cogitatio*), nor moral self-scrutiny (*meditatio*), important as those are, but a worshipful delight in the God of creation, the Logos incarnated for our redemption. The integration of faith and learning leads to this sort of contemplation, to a piety that furthers moral and spiritual development and inspires the pursuit of truth.

What then do these historical emphases of Christian higher education say about building the Christian academy today? They warn us about premature specialization and the increasingly utilitarian view of education. They tell us to reemphasize the liberal arts, their formative role, their transferable skills, the critical thinking they teach, their storehouse of wisdom, the substance they give to worldview thinking, the basis and the broad context they provide for the professions and other specialized occupations, the questions they ask about the meaning and purpose of life and about truth and beauty and goodness.

They tell us that student formation must be more intentional, that it depends in large measure on the caring mentor who befriends a student, takes interest in his spiritual life as well as his social and extracurricular activities, sees benefits to be derived and stumbling blocks to avoid and advises accordingly, who recognizes the student's strengths and weaknesses as well as his gifts, who models work as service and believes that who we are is more important than what we do. We need to talk about the characteristic temptations that professionals and students face in their fields of service, and about the particular virtues they need: intellectual modesty for philosophy majors, altruism for business majors. We need to build that kind of community on campus and within departments, communities of faith and character and learning, supportive communities that model appropriate virtues.

The historical emphasis on the unity of truth reminds us that Christian scholarship is not the "outrageous idea" that some of our secular counterparts suppose, and that Christian perspectives are specially needed in academia today. The threefold Logos theology and the creation mandate should ground our thinking not only about education, but about art and science, technology and business and all the professions, and indeed about all of life. We need Christian thinking not only about foundational questions, but also about points of tension between faith and knowledge, about theoretical concepts within a discipline, about the ethical issues new knowledge poses. We need multidisciplinary Christian reflection on crucial issues that confront us in the twenty-first century. Scholasticism provides an excellent model for creative minds with intellectual rigor, professional expertise, and an informed faith. We need to work at that quality of thinking now if we are to find it in the next generation of college teachers, individuals now in college themselves.

The doxological emphasis on contemplation currently receives the least attention of the four. Ours is a more activist and pragmatic society that has lost interest in theological reflection and perhaps in the art of worship itself. It has been a long time since I last heard a sermon on God's attribute of wisdom or power or even goodness, yet they were the foci of monastic doxologies. Without reflection on the nature of God, worship is thin. Yet the particular distinctive of collegiate worship should surely be its thoughtfulness; how can this be recaptured? An obvious first step is to relate college chapel to the classroom, whereas too often "chapel" has become what one former administrator calls "the least integrated time of the week." We need to recover the habit of contemplative learning that glorifies God in all the arts and sciences, and to acknowledge that in him are "all the treasures of wisdom and knowledge." When liberal learning is offered to God, it becomes an act of worship.

In short, we must return to the liberal arts. We must build community and reintroduce the *paidagogus*. Christian scholarship must be cultivated, and we must focus on the theological foundations of learning.

Arnold Nash's worldwide order of Christian scholars has not yet been formed, as Mark Noll's *Scandal of the Evangelical Mind*[19] makes clear. But in addition to the nearly one hundred evangelical liberal arts colleges in the Council for Christian Colleges and Universities (which emphasizes the integration of faith, learning, and living), the larger Christian academy is represented as it was in previous centuries by colleges and universities in other Christian traditions, by faithful teachers and scholars in secular institutions in this and other lands, and by organizations committed to supporting Christian scholarship and nurturing the next gen-

19. Mark A. Noll, *The Scandal of the Evangelical Mind* (Grand Rapids: Eerdmans, 1994).

eration who will take our place.[20] Theirs is the task of building the Christian academy now and for the future.

---

20. I have in mind the variety of institutions represented by Richard Hughes and William Adrian in *Models for Christian Higher Education* (Grand Rapids: Eerdmans, 1997), and the Lilly network of church-related colleges, the Pew Evangelical Scholarly Initiative, The Institute for Advanced Christian Studies, the Council of Christian Scholarly Societies (embracing most disciplinary organizations), and I.V.C.F. faculty and graduate student ministries.

Index